EVERYTHING I WISH I KNEW ABOUT MONEY THAT WASN'T TAUGHT IN SCHOOL

PAUL HUMPHREY

MERI HUMPHREY

with

BRIAN CULP

ABOUT THE BOOK

These days being a teenager means more than thinking about the next big game, or homecoming dance, or senior year. You'll spend your lifetime learning about adulting things like finance, credit and investing. The best time to take a proactive role in managing your money is while you are young and can establish solid financial practices that will last a lifetime.

Explore topics like budgets, assets, credit cards, credit scores, the secrets to turning small investments into big dollars, and how inflation and the Consumer Price Index (yeah—that's a thing) could affect all your buying decisions. These are all important things to know while thinking about buying that first car or saving for college. By using the easy concepts, practices and tips we outline in this book, you'll learn how to be a millionaire way down the road when you are ready to retire. Because even though you might be young, it's never too early to prepare for a financially secure future.

ACKNOWLEDGMENTS

Without the help of many friends, this book would not be complete. Many hours were spent addressing the content and organization. For all of their help, I would like to acknowledge:

1. Linda Madsen
2. Tim Klinkhammer
3. Lesa Stegner
4. Stev Stegner
5. Jeff Gauvin
6. Dan Hames
7. Christopher Luger
8. Chris Stauner

Paul Humphrey, CFEd® & Founder
Humphrey Financial, LLC

255 South Shore Drive
Forest Lake, MN 55025

phone: 952.201.0146
 email: paul@humphreyfinancial.com
fax: 651.272.5277

CHAPTER ONE

TAKING A PROACTIVE ROLE IN MANAGING YOUR FINANCES

We'll start things with a quick story.

Unfortunately, it doesn't have a happy ending.

About four years ago, we had a family friend who sent their 18-year-old son to an elite college not too far from where we live. By the time he was "finished" with college, and yes, we're using air quotes around the word "finished" because in many ways, college had finished with him, the son had accrued over **$130,000 in debt.**

What's more, his degree had prepared him for a profession whose workers get paid a typical entry-level salary of about $40,000 a year.

To be clear: we think the profession in question is *extremely* worthwhile, and from talking to others in this field, the actual work is deeply satisfying. Unfortunately, the work just doesn't pay all that much relative to the value it provides to society as a whole.

As we will be exploring in the lessons to follow, $40,000 per year isn't going to leave much over at the end of the month to be able to service much in the way of debt, much less a debt that has ballooned to the six figures plus the price of a new car; a debt that can't be escaped even through the legal mechanism of bankruptcy.

To compound matters, this young man's parents had *co-signed* on the loans needed to pay for the elite college, meaning that if the son could not pay back the loan, creditors could pursue his parents for the money owed. We will talk more about what co-signing is later, but typically co-signers guarantee loans will be repaid by promising creditors their assets if balances aren't paid – these can be things like life savings, or even the very house the co-signers live in. Lesson one: never, *ever* cosign without understanding what that means.

We won't share all the details of what happened next, but you can probably imagine most of it easily enough. Suffice to say that the emotional stress caused by the financial stress – not to mention the actual economic toll extracted from the parents – was an extremely destructive force that swept through the lives of both the young man and his parents.

As mentioned, it has now been four years since the son went off to college, full of hope and energy for the future before him, carrying a transcript full of good test scores and an even better GPA, and to this day, both the son and his family have yet to recover.

The lesson that we can take from this story is that being smart and *being smart with money* are two very different things. Now, life is extraordinarily complex, and the factors that cause us to make one decision versus another are unique to the individual – after all, not everyone who borrows $130,000 to attend school ends up with the same outcome as our friend's son – but in our view, much of the turmoil that has swept through this particular family could have been avoided had the son – and his parents for that matter – possessed a better understanding of personal finance.

Maybe the fate could have been prevented with the right *book*.

Obviously, following our friend's son so closely, and seeing the suffering his family has endured, has had a profound effect on the both of us. It has been a major influence on our desire to compile the book you now hold in your hands. Our main objective is to help you avoid a similar outcome.

Our hope is that this book keeps you from becoming the next son or daughter whose financial life spins out of control.

The Benefits of Personal Finance

So, we've laid out our motivations. But let's get to a more important issue: **you.**

As in, why are *you* reading this book?

We've both been in school, so we know that sometimes you can skate by a class or two with – cough, cough – less than optimal effort (especially some of those elective classes, right?). I mean, you can always try to get notes from another classmate and muddle your way through.

Hey, we've been there: sometimes D is for diploma.

On the other hand, since this is probably *not* required curriculum for your school, we're guessing you're not even getting this book assigned in the first place if you don't have at least a passing interest in the material.

So, what we really mean is, *should* you read this book?

The answer, of course, is a resounding yes. You should.

And the reason is because of the *benefits* you get from taking a more proactive role in managing your finances.

It's hard to overstate the impact this information might have on the rest of your life. After all, your financial situation could affect where you go to college, *if* you go to college, how much debt you'll have when you leave college, where you'll live after graduating from college (or not graduating), what kind of place you'll live in, all of which can have a dramatic impact on your social circle, and even perhaps influence whom you end up with as a life partner.

What we're saying is that virtually *every aspect* of your life – even matters that on the surface are more spiritual in nature – will eventually be impacted by your financial circumstances. For example, that yoga mat won't pay for itself. And the church, mosque, or synagogue you attend is eventually going to ask for some kind of financial gift so they have the means to carry out their mission.

Being in control of your finances – and please note that we are not saying "wealthy" here, but rather just knowing *where* and *why* your money is being spent – will give you a sense of independence, responsibility, and autonomy that few other things can provide at this early stage of your adulthood.

And remember, we're saying this as former teens. We're saying this as former teens who, in one case, left home without even knowing about a savings account. Crazy, right?

So, we write from a place of deep empathy when we say that ignorance about matters of personal finance can be deeply unsettling for someone trying on the clothing of adulthood for the first time.

In fact, ignorance about financial matters can sometimes leave grown adults (you) feeling like little children.

Speaking of children, another motivating factor in creating this book is that it has always boggled our minds that we're exposed to so many different academic disciplines during our childhood and early teen years, and yet virtually nothing in the way of finance. Throughout our early years, we learn about things such as the parts of speech, the planets in the solar system, and how to divide small numbers into much larger ones. As we progress towards high school, we are exposed to areas of human understanding as varied as the themes explored in Shakespearian plays, the DNA composition of Bonobo monkeys, the inner workings of an automobile engine, the computer code that will create an iPhone app, or a thousand other items of scholarship. When you think about it, by the time we're ready to leave high school, we've been exposed to a staggering amount of information.

But unless you were raised by parents who took a personal interest in teaching you about money stuff, you leave high school with all of the personal finance aptitude of a toddler who struggles to put on a button-down shirt for the first time. When it comes to finances, we're grown adults, and most of us can barely get dressed.

This book was designed to address what we view as one of the major downfalls of the current educational curriculum, especially at the high school level. We've written it because we're all going to make money and spend money thorough the course of our lives.

So that leaves us with three big questions that we have to answer about that money.

The Three Big Questions

When you get right down to it, the components that go into most every single personal financial plan – including plans for young adults – are fairly simple.

Even better, these components reveal themselves naturally once we provide the answers to three basic questions:

1. Where do I get my money, and how much is it?
2. What do I want to use the money for?
3. How will I save and spend money so that I can reach my goal?

These answer to these three questions provides the foundation for much of what's to follow in this book. We will explore each of these topics in more detail as we continue, but each is worth a brief introduction here.

Where do You Get Your Money?

Making massive amounts of money in your teen years has never been easier.

All you have to do is get your own reality TV show on the E! network and then have advertisers make media buys on all of that programming. Alternatively, you can create your own makeup channel on YouTube (and Instagram, of course) and have about 10 million subscribers, product sponsorships, and appearance fees at various conventions and mall openings across the nation.

See? Couldn't be easier.

Wait. Are you saying you *don't* have these things?

Oh. OK, fine. Then I guess this question addresses how everyone whose last name isn't Kardashian has to come up with ways to pay for things like gas, food, clothing, transportation, and, hmm… seems like I'm missing something…

Oh yeah! College! They charge you to take classes at college now. Unless you want to do your college studies in Norway, that is. Seriously. College is free in Norway. And Germany. Free, even for Americans. No, seriously… it's worth looking into.

So where does someone in their late teenage years obtain the funds they need to achieve their financial objectives?

Essentially, a teen's income comes from one of two activities:

1. Having an **allowance.**
2. Working at a **job.**

The word we're defining here is **income.**

To obtain an income, teens either work at a job and receive a paycheck, or they need to work at the job of going to school and participating in other activities, and then receive a gift from their parents. In some cases, a teen gets income from both sources.

In later chapters we'll identify some of the potential sources of that income, and how you might maximize your weekly or monthly pay.

What Do I Want to Use the Money for?

So now that we have money, what are we going to do with the money? Well, let's consider our options. We could:

1) stuff it in a coffee can and bury it in the back yard,

2) hide it under the mattress, or

3) use it for some immediate or future benefit.

Personally, we vote for option #3.

To put it bluntly, young adulthood is a time to be selfish. It's about creating the future that you want to live in. There will be plenty of time to invite others into the world you're building during your early adult years. (Most of the time, you'll also end up asking a few people to *leave* the world you're trying to create, although that's a topic for another book.)

The money you have and the plans that you make are for your benefit, and, with rare exception, yours alone.

And don't worry: the goals you set for your money only have to be defined in the most general of terms. You don't have to decide just yet *where* you want to attend college, or go to a trade school, or purchase an automobile, but rather that you simply *want* to attend college, or a trade school, or buy that car that will get you back and forth to work and school.

Kind of like when you're traveling, you pick the destination first (the beach!), and then decide on the specific activities later on (surfing on Friday morning!).

How Will I Save and Spend to Reach My Goal?

OK. Now that we have a concept of what money we have, and what we want to use it for, it's time to get to the execution part.

What we're looking for here is the **plan.**

Without some kind of plan or blueprint for how to get from where you are now to where you want to be – you'll find yourself asking a very different question at the end of every month, and unfortunately, the question will sound like this:

"Hey, what just happened to all my money?"

If you have a plan, your **money** has a purpose.

If you have a plan, your **work** has a purpose.

If you have a plan, **you** have a purpose.

When you have a purpose for your studies, work and savings, you'll quickly realize how much better life is; how much less over-whelming it is to deal with the Big Three money questions, rather than the one that starts with, "What just happened…?"

Facing the question of "What just happened?" can leave even

the smartest among us feeling like an idiot. The good news, however, is that having a plan for our money can be liberating.

It can *allow* us the freedom of being an idiot in the first place.

Be an Idiot. With a Plan.

Ever heard of someone named T. Boone Pickens?

If you haven't, here's the brief bio: Pickens grew up in Amarillo, Texas, and then attended Texas A&M University on a basketball scholarship. However, Texas A&M eliminated Pickens' scholarship after his freshman year, which then forced him to transfer to Oklahoma A&M, which we know today as Oklahoma State University.

And, seeing as the football stadium where the Oklahoma State Cowboys play in is now named after Pickens, getting cut from the basketball team at Texas A&M didn't pan out too well for the Aggies, at least in terms of athletic department fundraising. (It worked out great for the Cowboys, though.)

But that's not the important part of why we mention T. Boone Pickens here. What's more important is a quote of his which has become somewhat famous, one that he gave during congressional testimony (and in subsequent public interviews) sometime in 2008, during a time when gas prices were spiking to record highs.

Here it is:

"A fool with a plan can beat a genius with no plan."

It's a bit ironic that Pickens is known for this quote, as he was apparently quoting from advice his *father* had given him when he was a young man just starting out in the oil business.

What's more, it wasn't even technically meant as advice. At the time, Pickens was being *scolded* by his parents. Hard as it might be to believe, parents sometimes give their offspring a righteous chewing out.

The *full* quote that Pickens heard from his father was this:

"You'd better get a plan. A fool with a plan can beat a genius with no plan. Your mother and I think we have a fool with no plan."

Now, is the fact that Pickens has made a fortune in oil and energy a result of great planning, or great luck? Drilling oil wells involves a massive amount of risk, and many people and companies have gone bankrupt because of oil wells that didn't pan out, so we want to be nuanced with our analysis of Mr. Pickens.

Our view is that it's both. He was lucky, and he had a solid plan.

Our view is that his planning created the environment whereby he *could* get lucky. Our view is that Pickens is living proof of the other planning aphorism with which you may already be familiar:

Luck is where planning meets opportunity.

In fact, the role of planning is so significant for Mr. Pickens that he has become somewhat famous for the announcement of a major energy policy proposal called the **Pickens Plan,** and it's one that incorporates more than a bit of irony for someone who made his fiscal bones drilling for oil. The Pickens Plan calls for a radical reduction in the United States dependency on foreign energy by introducing alternatives to oil, including wind and solar.

If you've ever driven across the vast expanses of western Texas, Oklahoma, or western Kansas, you may have even seen aspects of the Pickens Plan in action in the form of giant windmills generating electricity in a wind corridor that stretches from northern Texas all the way to the Canada - U.S. border.

In any event, one of the things that we can all learn from the Pickens Plan is that it has a clearly stated goal, which is to help the U.S. become energy independent. When it comes to finances in early adulthood, the task of crafting a solid plan is made much easier once we know the objectives our plan supports.

And if it sounds like we had a firm grasp on all of these issues when we were sitting at high school desks, then we have a confession to make before proceeding.

A Shocking Confession

You may have a very difficult time believing this, but both of the authors of this book empathize with the daily struggles – both internal and external – of being a teenager because of this one simple fact.

One time, many years ago, both of us were teenagers ourselves.

Yes, hard to fathom.

But we know what it's like to make impulsive decisions, to fall on our faces, to be uncertain of what the world has in store for us, and to be uncertain about how on earth we'll navigate the many years of adulthood in front of us. We can empathize with feeling ashamed – or even like idiots – when dealing with money issues.

We know what it's like to be *scared.*

One of the overriding impulses for creating this project was to help you learn from some of the many mistakes we've made during the time of life you're in right now. What kind of mistakes and background are we talking about here?

Let's take a brief moment to introduce the two mistake-prone former teenagers who are writing this book.

Paul Humphrey

I grew up in St. Paul, Minnesota, the oldest in a family of three. As the oldest child in the family, I look back on my early adulthood as a time where I was training my parents for my other siblings to follow.

For example, I have vivid memories of trying to get my driver's license. I was 16, and ready to get my license, and my parents dragged their feet for almost a year while I bugged them almost daily. I wanted to get a car, and then use the car to get to work, and then eventually to college. It wasn't until I was almost 17 when I finally got my license.

But when it was time for my younger brother? My folks couldn't have been more accommodating. Maybe my folks were just scared at the thought of their son out driving around and risking life and limb – and as a parent myself, I can understand this apprehension – but my folks probably learned from me that when one of their teens was ready to drive, then it wasn't worth the weekly pleading and prodding to stall.

My mentality from a very early age is that I have fought and scraped for every little thing I could get. But perhaps this is the lot in life that many eldest siblings face. If you're an oldest yourself, perhaps you understand exactly the situation I was in.

I attended the University of Minnesota and graduated with a degree in mechanical engineering. I then spent the next 20 years traveling all over the world (traveling too much, in fact) fixing and helping install temperature control infrastructure for companies like Honeywell, Trane, and McQuay.

I also worked all through college, washing dishes and making food in other fraternity houses simply for food, and in the U of M repair shop department for cash, in order to <u>pay</u> for that college education. In the end, I was able to graduate without any debt. This is something that gave me a sense of accomplishment then, and something that I still look back on with pride today. (I do realize that college was considerably less expensive back then.)

After 20 years as a mechanical engineer, my department was reassigned to offices in Louisville, Kentucky, except I didn't want to go. I had reached my limit with travel, my life was in Minnesota, and I wanted to stay. My company footed the bill for one of those strengths finder tests you might have taken at the urging of your guidance counselor, and the assessment suggested that I was well-suited for either pharmaceutical sales or financial planning. And since I wasn't very good with pronouncing big words like the names of prescription drugs, I ended up selecting option B when changing careers, became a Financial Advisor, and have never looked back.

As I recall the days of my early adulthood, one thing that certainly worked in my favor was my ability to plan and to focus, and in writing this book, I'm hoping that you can learn from some of my experiences in that department. About the only regret I have in my professional life is that I didn't get into the business of financial planning sooner.

In short, I love what I do, and what I do is help people navigate the often-choppy waters of personal finance.

Meri Humphrey

When I moved out of the house at age 18, I was hardly ready for the transition to adulthood.

Specifically, my mother paid my rent.

Here I was, thinking I was some kind of capital-A Adult, thinking that I was ready to be out on my own, and I couldn't figure out how to keep a roof over my head for *one* month! I was working at a restaurant making little more than minimum wage (which was about a $1.50 an hour back then), and as I look back on it now, it's not without some sense of embarrassment. Clearly, I was not ready to be out on my own.

The outward appearance I presented to the world was that of an independent, responsible adult. But inside, I knew that was not the case, and that internal conflict ate away at my confidence. I felt dependent on others, and that's because I *was*.

How did that eventually manifest itself? I gave up on many of my life's goals, only picking them back up again many years later. And in terms of money? Ha! I didn't really start to learn much about finances until I had teenagers of my own.

So yes, I've been young, and dumb, and I've been irresponsible when it comes to matters of personal finance. In many ways, I'm still learning. I eventually went back to school and earned my degree in education in 1998, and then just... *kept* going to school. I eventually earned my master's degree in 2005, and have been in the classroom from September to May ever since, like many of you.

Who knew learning could be so much fun?

I'm proud of what I've done in the classroom, both as an adult student and as a teacher – and certainly prouder of my recent classroom accomplishments than I am of my earlier stumbles. Both, however, have shaped the person I am today, so in most regards, I am grateful for both experiences.

My objective in working on this project is to help you avoid some of the difficulties I experienced that resulted from my own uninformed decisions.

CHAPTER TWO

WHAT'S YOUR GOAL?

Set the Goal

So, let's practice.

We'll practice the art of personal finance by setting a *goal*, and then developing a *plan* to move us towards that goal.

High school is a time for practice – for choir practice to develop a better understanding of music and our singing skills, for basketball practice where we learn more about working with a team, and turning abstract instructions into physical action, and most importantly, about increasing blood flow to the brain so you can improve cognition and strategic thinking. (You thought we were going to say, "Get better at basketball." A secondary benefit of being on the basketball team, to be sure.)

Heck, even *homework* is practice. You spend time in the evening learning Newton's Laws of Motion to understand that things tend to drop to the ground (when released from just a short distance from the Earth's surface, that is).

In this chapter, we're going to begin the *practice* of sound financial management by selecting a goal that we're going to work and save for.

But don't worry, we'll keep this very simple: Just picture something you want to buy that you don't have today. We want to make the goal both **specific** and **attainable** while you're reading this book, so let's not make it something that's either abstract – saving for college, for example – or something that's going to take years of effort – a new Tesla.

If we do it right, we can apply these strategies to other goals we have later in life (or just goals for next semester). Here are a few ideas to get you started:

- A pair of sick new Uggs.
- A dope new Kavu backpack.
- A fine new phone cover.
- A pair of Beats or AirPods that are so money.
- A Gucci Starbucks gift card.
- A puppy. (Your parents will *love* this idea!)

So, got your goal in mind? Great. Keep it there until we reach the end of the chapter. (Don't make it a puppy, please.) Have we used all the words that will make us sound like we're cool old people? (You're saying we're not? Our secret is out, I guess.)

And speaking of reaching for things, let's now discuss how you'll acquire the income needed to reach your target.

Income: Your Vehicle to Your Goal

When you're in your teens, your *profession* is to be a student. And profession is absolutely the right word for it. You're in school 30-50 hours per week, depending on your involvement in school-sponsored activities, and anything you do for 30-50 hours a week is your full-time job. And that's before we even get to the subject of homework.

If you don't believe me, just ask your teachers why they show up to the same building you do between 7 a.m. to about 3 or 4 p.m., five days a week. After they ask, "Why are you asking?" they'll answer, "Because it's my job."

So, not only is it your *job* and your *responsibility* to attend school and learn as much as you can that will hopefully prepare you for the future you, but it's also legally *required*. I know. Bummer.

In any event, the other unfortunate part of being legally required to have "student" as an occupation is that being a student doesn't pay very well. Scratch that. It doesn't pay at all, or at least not while we're still in high school. Once we hit college, being a full-time student (or student athlete) can certainly generate benefits that are as good as income.

But for now, we'll just have to deal with the fact that as a high school student, we'll have to obtain the income needed to fuel our goals by other means than studying really hard in class.

As we mentioned in the first chapter, the income you receive – answering one of our Big Three questions – will come from one of two sources:

1. Having an **allowance.**
2. Working at a **job.**

Let's begin with the topic of allowances. Don't have an allowance? That's OK. We'll deal with working in just a bit. But maybe this section can help you make the case to your folks. Every little bit can help you closer to your goal.

An Allowance

Parents can be so awful when it comes to allowances. And by awful, we mean that they can be awful in how they give out allowances, which usually takes one of these forms:

- Handing a kid/teen a $20 bill when they want to see a movie.
- Handing a kid/teen a credit card that's *only* to be used for gas or emergencies. (Yeah, right… those hot dogs and 20-ounce energy drinks at the local Quickie Mart don't exactly count as gas, but we won't tell if you don't tell.)
- Giving a kid/teen $20 bucks every Sunday night just for remembering to breathe over the past week, an

allowance plan which the parents will forget about after two Sundays, and then get testy when you try to very politely remind them, and so it's not worth the hassle. Instead, you'll just make their lives hell next time you're in the store and want a new pair of Birks.

In other words, parents rarely give any thought to the question of **why**.

As in, why is the parent just giving the kid money?

Actually, this is where you might be able to help. Whether or not an allowance is currently a part of your financial picture, we challenge you to at least have a discussion with your folks about the possibility. We promise, most parents are very reasonable people when addressed with courtesy and respect. (We said most of them.)

Our main suggestion is to **treat allowances like a work paycheck,** because as we just mentioned earlier in the chapter, that's really what it is. It can be viewed as your wages for being a full-time student.

If it helps, start the conversation around allowances with a question or two. For example, what are your parents' reasons for having an allowance? Do they want you to learn fiscal responsibility? Do they want you to spend or save your money wisely? Learn about a solid work ethic, or the value of a dollar?

In short, ask you parents about what's motivating them to give you an allowance (or not give you one; these can be valuable conversations as well). You may not agree with their reasoning, but at least you'll know that there's been some thinking behind their decision(s). And by asking them to talk through their thought process, you may find there is room for improvement and/or change.

In some cases, parents who give (or don't give) an allowance may not have given it much thought at all. It's just something their own parents did (or didn't do) for them.

And as much as you might dread a conversation about finance

with your parents, you might be pleasantly surprised by the response you receive. Most of the parents we know are absolutely *thrilled* when their kids show any inclination towards "adulting."

You might be even more pleasantly surprised by the response when you tie the discussion of allowance into a discussion of saving for a goal. If you tell your folks that you're saving up for something specific, and want to follow a spending and savings *plan* (there's that word again) rather than just hit them up for money once in a while, our view is that you've just dramatically increased your odds for success.

In fact, parents who've never even *considered* an allowance might suddenly see the value in a small investment every two weeks in exchange for you doing your part – by being the best full-time student you can be. Parents who are approached with a "paycheck" model – especially if it's something that can be used in place of constant requests for a $20 to go see a show, or to fill the car with gas.

There are actually several different approaches parents and kids can agree will work for a particular situation. So, depending on how the conversation goes, you can suggest one of the following allowance strategies.

Approach 1. A Paycheck for Going to School

This is the most straightforward approach.

With this strategy, your folks decide on a salary for being a full-time student who also participates in orchestra, or cheerleading, or drama, or sometimes all of the above. You get paid every two weeks with either a paycheck that you deposit in your checking and savings accounts, or, easier still, via automatic deposits. In today's world, setting up automatic deposits and withdrawals takes just a minute or two.

If compromise is needed, you and your folks can suggest a sliding scale that fluctuates depending on what outside activities you're involved in. If doing your part in school and attending school play rehearsals every night, you get one amount. If simply going to school and riding the bus home every afternoon, perhaps another smaller amount, since you'd have more time to supplement that income.

Approach 2. Earn the Allowance by Doing Work

With this approach, the allowance is tailored to the work being done to earn it. For example, you can suggest a list of household chores and assign a set dollar amount to each one. The more work you do, the more money you will earn.

Just like real life, huh? For this reason, parents whose response to allowance is, "We don't give you an allowance because we want you to learn the value of work," might be especially receptive to this suggestion.

You work, you get paid. For best results, we suggest that you include a few of the duties that are normally left to your parents. We also suggest that you get close – yet offer a discount – to the going rate for similar services.

Here are a few ideas:

- Wash the family car for $15. (It would cost $15-$20 at a car wash.)
- Mow the lawn for $20, or more if it's a big yard. (You can call lawn and landscape companies to get an idea of what your folks would need to pay someone else to do the work.)
- Do a thorough house/apartment cleaning that takes most of a day for $100 or more, depending on the size of the house/apartment. (You can decide on a per room rate, perhaps.) Trust us, your folks want *something* cleaned – the garage, the grill, the gutters. Something.

If you encounter parental pushback on these suggestions, you might tell them that you're willing to work hard, and earn a paycheck, but someone's gonna have to mow the yard while you're out bagging groceries for $10/hour.

Keep it respectful. Show them the numbers. Show them the *value* of hiring you to do household chores in exchange for a paycheck. Can they get a top-to-bottom, once-a-month house cleaning from you for $50 less than they could from a professional service? Again, all parents are old, but most parents are not idiots – we're former idiots.

And, if you do get a hard "pass" on these ideas, then *thank* your folks for thinking it over and offer to pitch in around the house anyway.[1] Show gratitude. Life won't give you everything you want all the time, and your parents don't *have* to give you money just for being a contributing member of the household. The roof over your head at night doesn't pay for itself, after all. If you need to get a job to make money, so be it. Welcome to real life.

Approach 3. Getting Paid for Grades

This is sort of a hybrid between getting paid for being a full-time student and getting paid for doing work. We do understand that working life is ultimately about performance – if you get a job, you have to show up and keep performing well to keep that job, and thus that income – but that said, we're not particular fans of this approach.

Here's our thinking: yes, offering a cash incentive *can* encourage you to work harder in school, you may end up becoming more focused on the prize than the actual learning. When it comes to education, you're better served by actually *wanting* to learn – by actually loving the process of learning – than by mindlessly plowing through your homework so you can claim a few dollars at the end of the week.

What's more, once the cash incentive for grades is removed, as it usually is in college, it can train the student to slack off academically at a time where you can least afford to. We'll go into this in much more detail later in the book, but the cost of a college education today makes the stakes higher than ever before. In other words, college is not exactly a great time to figure out whether you're studying because you really like learning, or because you really like cash prizes.

However, if it's cash you truly seek – as eventually all of us will – then we need to turn our attention to employment.

Having a Job

Of course, we can also work and save towards our goal – *still have that goal in mind?* – by seeking out an old-fashioned job. Almost all teenagers can benefit from employment experience as they are growing up.

Seeking summer employment is a part of many teenagers' lives, and the benefits of working in the summer are self-evident. But the issue before us is whether to work in the fall, winter, and spring – during the months when students are still taking classes, doing homework, and getting ready for homecoming dances.

We're going to be really wishy-washy here and say that whether or not a job is right for you will depend on your individual circumstances. Here are some pros and cons to consider when thinking it over and/or talking it over with your parents.

Why You Should Work While in School

There are some compelling reasons why you might consider working, even while attending high school full time. Here are a few:

- To learn work skills that will serve you well in college and prepare you for a career.
- To gain confidence, independence, and to learn responsible money management skills.
- To do better in school. Students who work between 10 to 15 hours a week during the school year *tend to have higher grades* than those who don't work.

Why You Should Not Work While in School

Of course, washing dishes at the local bar until midnight on a Tuesday is probably not good for the long-term health of a high school student, either. Here are some reasons why working might not be such a great idea while trying to ace U.S. History:

- Students who work more than 15 to 20 hours a week typically have lower grades than their peers.
- Working too many hours makes it more difficult to keep up extracurricular activities and social relationships.
- Some studies that have found that teens working long hours are more likely to engage in such risky activities as using illegal drugs or alcohol.

Can You Even Work While in School?

Wait. Is it even legal to work?

Aren't there child labor laws against kids working while in school or something? I remember something about that in my U.S. History class. Or maybe it was English. Didn't Upton Sinclair write about child labor?

The short answer is that yes, there are (now) federal employment laws that mandate certain restrictions on work for teenagers. (And work restrictions for adults for that matter. It's illegal to discriminate, for example. With some caveats, it's illegal to require people to work overtime without paying them an overtime wage.)

With that, here are legal issues that apply to teens:

- Children younger than age 14 are restricted to delivering newspapers, working in a non-hazardous business owned by a parent, baby-sitting or doing other minor domestic chores in a private home, or performing on stage, screen or radio. They may work only between 7 a.m. and 7 p.m. during the school year and until 9 p.m. in the summer.
- At ages 14 and 15, teens may work at non-hazardous

jobs for three hours on school days, eight hours on non-school days, 18 hours during a school week, and 40 hours during a non-school week.
- At ages 16 and 17, teens may perform any non-hazardous job for any number of hours.

So, can you work 40 hours a week while you're a junior in high school? Yes.

Do we advise it? No.

What about when you're a senior and you're age 18? Can you do it then?

Listen, you're a grown adult when you're age 18, at least in the eyes of the law.[2] You can work all you want and live in in a van down by the river, leaving only to drive to casinos where the legal gambling age is 18.

But we don't advise that, either.

We won't presume to say whether working or not is a good answer to your situation. Even if you decide that work isn't or can't work for your school situation – you're on the school baseball team and it's spring, for example – then you should still be able to squeeze in a few hours of W-2 employment on weekends somewhere. Grocery and home improvement stores will want weekend help.

But hey, what's the alternative? Unless your baseball career is going to end up with you being drafted by an MLB team this June, then eventually you're going to run out of baseball practices, and you'll need income from somewhere. You can start with 4 hours every Sunday at the local grocery store.

It's not much, but it counts.

The biggest case the two of us can make for seeking out employment while you're still in high school is really the same reason this book exists: once you start to make your very own money, the real lessons about personal finance can begin.

In other words, nothing is a better teacher than experience, and once you have the experience of making, spending, and saving money, it's just not all that practical to learn about responsible money management. There's simply little benefit in it.

After all, your parents can sit you down in front of PBS's *Wall Street Week* when you're 7-years old, but so what? You're freaking seven. You don't have a brokerage account. So, it doesn't matter. Because you're seven.

However, when you're 17, there are some benefits to personal finance that are much more immediate. When you're 17, you can start contributing to your car expenses, your college fund, and your entertainment expenses. When you're 17, you can have a much greater appreciation of just how much things like food, gas and school cost.

As a final note, some kind of combination works in most situations as well – an allowance while in school and extracurricular activities, a paycheck from an employer when not.

These are small steps on a much larger journey.

CHAPTER THREE

NOT YOUR FATHER'S HOME ECONOMICS CLASS

The First Steps Towards Your Goal

Paul: You don't have to be a financial planner to understand the importance of concepts like money, budgeting, or investing.

It just seems that way sometimes.

And even though I'm now a financial planner, I had no idea about most of the concepts that we'll look at in this chapter while I was in high school. Or in college. Or really during the first several years while I was working as an engineer. So just by reading this book, you're getting a valuable overview about financial concepts and products that will – unless you plan on living in a treehouse in the woods for the rest of your life – have a profound impact on you and your loved ones.

Don't believe me? Let me give you just a few top-of-the-head examples of how your management of finances really becomes a discussion of how you manage your life.

- Whether or not you can afford to attend college or a

technical college – in person or online – will impact your life.
- Whether or not you will have to take out loans to finance that college or technical education will impact your life.
- Whether or not you qualify for a mortgage will impact your life.
- How much money you save out of monthly paychecks will impact your life.
- How you invest your money will impact your life.
- Whether or not you pay the obligations you take on will impact your life.

SCARED NOW? THRILLED ABOUT THE OPPORTUNITIES AHEAD?

Good.

Both emotions are appropriate, and both emotions are closely related. I promise you'll have many big moments big in your life where you feel both exhilarated and terrified at the same time.

MERI: AS YOU ALREADY KNOW, I AM <u>NOT</u> A FINANCIAL PLANNER, YET both Paul and I both possessed roughly equal amounts of understanding about money during early adulthood.

The only thing that was remotely close to a financial concepts course offered by high schools back when Paul and I were your age was a course called "Home Economics," which I took during my junior year.

I have no idea what we covered in that class, nor do I recall my final grade (perhaps the two things are related). What I can share with you, however, is a list of things that were <u>not</u> covered. We never once spoke about:

- Credit scores
- Investing
- Interest on debt

- Compounding interest
- Student loans
- Buying a car

In a class with the word "economics" in its title, my recollection is that we never actually discussed economic issues that would affect teenagers or young adults in the real world.

Paul and I have spoken to many parents over the years, many of whom take it as a point of pride that they're able to have honest and open discussions with their kids. These are parents who have learned from the mistakes of their *own* parents, and thus don't shy away from direct conversations about things like the necessity of seatbelts, the benefits of exercise and a healthy diet, or the dangers of alcohol and substance abuse. When it comes to topics like these, parents today aren't afraid of tackling these difficult exchanges head-on and taking great pains to ensure they're presenting clear and factual information.

However, when it comes to the topic of money, this rarely seems to be the case.

We know this because we've asked parents what they say to their kids about money. It's actually quite funny to observe the reaction to this question. Parents who have few qualms about having "the talk" with their teenagers suddenly squirm and/or change the subject whenever "the talk" turns to financial matters.

Whenever the topic of money arises, even the most modern of parents can be guilty of avoiding or even outright lying to sidestep a more meaningful, and possibly more educational, conversation.

In fairness, there may be several good reasons for why parents today avoid conversations about money. For one, the topic of finance can produce a range of negative emotions not only for teenagers, but for adults as well. Words like "debt" and "credit card" and "budgeting" can invoke feelings of worry, guilt, anxiety, and stress. Perhaps conversations about money have already been the topic of too many uncomfortable dinner conversations, or even arguments between Mom and Dad. Perhaps parents simply feel that since they don't have a good grasp of financial concepts themselves, they're not equipped to have intelligent conversations with their children. Perhaps adults are wrestling with their own feelings of shame and guilt over how they've handled their own financial lives; maybe they're afraid that by opening up a conversation about money, they're also opening up the possibility of looking bad in front of their kids – of admitting that they, too, kind of make it up as they go.

So, let's fix that.

Let's first start by forgiving ourselves for our current state of financial know-how. Let's also agree not to judge based on past financial missteps.

Secondly, let's understand that you don't need a background in financial planning to understand the financial *concepts* the most impact your life. Regardless of your current comfort level with financial matters, your current level of income, or whatever mistakes you may have made previously, the lessons in this book will provide a roadmap so that you and your family can implement healthy financial principles throughout your life.

Lastly, we'll use that mindset of forgiveness to begin talking about the tools and resources available in today's financial world, the world that you will be entering a soon (if you're not already there) as a legal, functioning adult. Let's equip you with the information that can help you lead a successful, financially stable life once you leave behind the pep rallies, cafeteria food, and band practices of your youth.

If Paul and I could go back in time and develop a personal finance curriculum to teach our teenage selves, here are some of the essentials that we would've included in that Home Economics class that never existed. (Believe it or not, this was a time before PayPal. But don't worry: While our intentions may be many years old, the topics discussed here and throughout this book reflect our current realities.)

Budgets

We'll start with a quick discussion of budgets, even though it's not *necessarily* the most important concept introduced in this chapter. Don't get us wrong: Budgeting is very important, but in our view, it's not as vital right now as learning about the *concept* of compounding interest and the *tools* of credit.

Believe us: We understand that budgeting is something that most people dread. But when most people think of budgeting, they're really talking about tracking every dollar they spend. And even though one of us is a financial advisor and the other is married to one, we don't really enjoy the task of budgeting any more than you do.

So, we don't do it.

Well, not in the way that it's commonly thought of.

What we do instead is something we refer to as *strategic budgeting*. That is, we create a monthly financial plan to make sure a certain financial goal is met. (Sound familiar? If not, uh, please go back and read Chapter 2. Your friend didn't give you very good notes.)

The nice thing about this type of budgeting is that it doesn't require us to watch every single penny. We do review our end-of-month reports from bank and financial tracking apps, mind you – a subject we will discuss later on – but most of all, this strategic budgeting simply helps us achieve our goals and spend less over time.

The big takeaway here is that what budgeting does, and the reason we're introducing it first, is that it provides a framework against which we can better evaluate the other two items introduced in this chapter. For example, if you want to achieve your goal amount more quickly, you first need to assess your current financial standing, and create a plan for what money is spent on what items. And what did we say earlier about having a plan?

That's right: An idiot with a plan beats a genius without one.

And it will be like this for the rest of your life. If you are deciding whether or not you can afford a car payment (or better, setting aside a set amount every month so you can pay for that car in cash), you'll consult your budget. As you plan to pay back a potential student loan, you'll consult your budget. You'll get to practice with a budget at the end of this chapter.

The biggest reason budgeting is such an important first step in achieving your financial goals is that it is an exercise in setting **priorities** for your work, and thus your money. You've already defined a financial goal. Now, the budget can help you *see* just how important that goal is compared to other things you have going on in your life. The budget will help you move in the direction of the goal, rather than spinning your wheels, wondering where all that money went by the time you reach the next payday.

And there's no reason why the act of creating a budget should be met with the same enthusiasm most feel towards final exams. For students and adult-types alike, an effective budget can be very simple indeed. All you really need are two ingredients.

First, the budget must be **written** – either on paper or a spreadsheet. A budget in your head doesn't count. We're not trying to remember what to get at the grocery store, we're setting intentions for the dollars we earn. If you play sports, ask yourself if your coach simply describes the plays she wants you to execute, or whether she gets out a whiteboard and draws letters and symbols. If you play music, does your teacher tell you about which notes to play, or are the notes written down on bass and treble staffs? In all areas of life, plans are virtually meaningless unless they are committed to paper (even if the paper is digital).

Second, the budget lists out both your **income** (from sources such as work, loans, allowances, and so on), and your expected **expenses** (your books, rent, food, gas, savings, car payment, movie tickets, cell phone bill, etc.).

Once everything is listed out, subtract the total of your expenses from your income. The final number that you calculate should not be a negative number. If it is, you need to make some adjustments – either make more money, or cut some of your expenses.

The World's Simplest Budget

So, the good news is that budgeting should now be seen simply as an exercise in setting priorities. What's more important, saving for college or driving a car? Your budget will answer that question in terms that are hard to argue with. As we have seen and heard anecdotally in our own lives, if someone's App Store purchases are $70/month and you're only saving $50 towards your college expenses, then you're announcing to the world quite clearly which one is more important in your mind. Whether you choose to listen to this announcement and adjust behavior, of course, is up to you.

The even better news is that students *can* have it particularly easy when it comes to budgeting, because most students don't have to factor in common adult items such as mortgage payments, medical expenses, or electric bills.

The world's simplest budget contains just **three** items:

- Income
- Savings
- Spending money

That's it!

This is what we refer to as *excuse-free* budgeting. It eliminates any reasons for not setting aside a certain amount of money each month towards a financial goal.

The way it works is that you will have a portion of each paycheck automatically deposited into a savings or an investment account that you simply do not touch until you have achieved your goal amount. After that, you have the freedom to spend the remaining amount however you please.

We're hardly the first ones to articulate this concept. Some other personal finance types, most notably a personal finance author and TV personality by the name of David Bach, refers to this method as "paying yourself first." The idea is that you don't wait until the end of the month, or the end of the pay period, to see if you have money left over from the previous month or pay period. Instead, the money is automatically invested toward your goal before you get to spend a single cent.

This "pay yourself first" approach is excuse-free because once it's configured, you'll never "forget" to set aside your budgeted savings amount ever again the way you might have "forgotten" to turn in your last biology lab assignment.

At the end of the chapter, we'll practice with the world's easiest budget, and use that to automatically fund our goal amount.

Compounding Interest

Let's begin with the principle we consider the most important financial concept for anyone to learn. In our view, this is true for adults who are your parent's age, and it's *especially* true for people in their late teens and early 20s.

The principle of **compounding interest.**

If you stop reading this book tomorrow – if this is the last paragraph of the book you'll ever read – then we take some small comfort in the fact that we have at least exposed you to this financial principle, which is as follows:

Over time, money makes even more money.

Another way to think of compounding interest is that *time is your friend*. Compounding interest means that time will grow a very small pile of money into one that's so big that you almost won't be able to spend it all.

Let's walk through a quick example, using numbers that we might have generated for ourselves based on the assignment in the previous chapter.

If we were both young adults today, one of the things we might most want to save our money for would be a top-of-the-line smartphone. We imagine we would need to save about $1000 for that new smartphone. But, let's also assume that our parents have gifted us a smartphone when we turned 13 or 14 as many parents today seem to do. So instead, we have set our sights on something even less expensive – saving for a new iPad.

How much will we need for the new iPad?

$600.

Now, let's further assume that we anticipate that will take us 3 months to put aside enough money to purchase that iPad without using a credit card. Since it would take us three months to save $600, how much would we hypothetically be able to save over the course of an entire year?

$2400

Now, instead of buying that iPad, let's see what compounding interest could do with our iPad savings over the course of our adulthood.

Assuming you're 17 years old today, if you take those same numbers and plug them into a compound interest calculator at an 8% interest rate, by the time you reach age 60, **you would have almost $700,000.**

(Oh, and you can buy a lot of iPads with $700,000.)

A Quick Aside About the Cost of Smoking

We won't pretend to influence your decision about whether or not to take up cigarette smoking, or at least not from the health side of things. Hopefully, something like that will be covered in a health and/or biology class, and if not there, we trust there are plenty of resources on the health risks associated with smoking that can be accessed by the time you're done reading this paragraph.

What this aside is about is the potential *financial* impact of cigarettes. Something else that will set you back $200/month is a pack of cigarettes every day at $8 per pack. The difference between saving for an iPad and smoking, however, is that you're done saving for the iPad after three months. If you do three months of cigarettes, the odds are that you're going to be "saving" this amount every month for the rest of your (likely shortened) life.

So, as we've just seen, saving $200/month starting today can net you $700,000 by time you're 60, money you can use for iPads, or heck, maybe even a fleet of *flying* iPads by that time.

Alternatively, a pack per day smoking habit can *cost* you $700,000.

And that's before we pay for your lung cancer treatments and associated care, which can easily set you back another six figures.

And that's before we factor in the reduction in earning potential that's the result of you being sick for much of your 50s and dead before age 70. As two people who are in their 60s, we can tell you that we are not finished earning a monthly paycheck, thank you very much.

The bottom line is that your decision to get hooked on cigarettes today can easily cost you over a million dollars in lifetime earnings. Easily. And even if you don't spend that million on yourself, trust us that either your kids, your grandkids, or your favorite charity will be very grateful that you've chosen not to burn up your lifetime savings one Marlboro at a time. (If you're ever tempted, just visualize each ciggy wrapped in a $20 bill. In terms of your lifetime earnings, it might as well be.)

In other words, your decision not to smoke can be a *generational* decision. So, what's your decision? Are you going to keep and spend that money for yourself? Or, by choosing to smoke, are you going to pass it down to the grandkids of some cigarette executive?

The Most Valuable Asset

The point here is not to influence your decision about whether or not to purchase an iPad, or anything else you might have defined as your goal in the previous chapter. After all, an iPad can be a great tool in almost any profession, including being a full-time student, or a job that requires certain tools to effectively do the work. We needed a computer and word processing program to churn out this book, after all. (Oh, and if your goal was a carton of cigarettes, then perhaps it's time to reexamine your life priorities.)

Instead, the point here is to quickly illustrate the power that compounding interest has to turn relatively small amounts of money into massive piles of wealth later on in your life.

Why is this so significant? Because when you're young, what commodity do you have not very much of? Unless your last name is either Bieber or Kardashian, the answer is **money.** Unless you're one of these folks, the amounts of money you're able to save during the early portions of your wage-earning years is relatively small. (In fact, in a later chapter, we'll explain why having massive piles of money early in life makes it even more likely that someone will end up broke.)

But that's okay. It's okay because when you're young, what do you have lots of?

Time.

And **time is the more valuable asset.**

If you don't believe me, ask your parents – or heck, ask anyone around our age – which they'd rather have more of: Time or money?

Four out of 5 adults will say "time," and 1 out of 5 adults will lie right to your face.

Credit Cards

Awesome. You've now learned about the power of compounding interest.

But let's start out the discussion of credit cards with some bad news: you're not the only one who understands how compounding interest works. You know who else has an intimate knowledge of compounding interest?

Credit card companies.

And they leverage this knowledge to become very, very profitable.

It's especially important to understand the tool of credit *right now* because you're entering a phase in your life where you're going to have the ability to get your own credit card. Remember what we said about the freedom and responsibility that's associated with turning 18? One of those freedoms will include the potential to start buying items on credit.

Which can be great. And can also be devastating.

And because credit card companies understand the math of compounding interest so intimately, many of these businesses will be doing *everything they can* to make sure that the first credit card you use is the one they sell you. They will try to entice you with rewards like cashback for meeting certain spending thresholds.

The fact that many credit card companies offer – and by offer we mean advertise – travel point bonuses for spending several thousand dollars soon after you've opened an account is not by accident. Always remember that there are marketing professionals who are paid very well to know their target market and how to appeal to that audience. They know that today's younger generation puts a higher emphasis on experiences as status symbols rather than on things. They know that younger people spend a great deal of time, attention – and the money – trying to emulate the glamorous vacation images that are posted on Snapchat, Instagram, Facebook, and other social media platforms.

That's not to say that a credit card isn't a useful tool in a modern economy. If fact, there are many transactions in today's economy that will *require* a credit card. To take just one example, if you want to rent a car at the airport when starting off that dream vacation purchased with credit card sign-up bonus points, you'll actually *need* that credit card to make a reservation (a fact which, again, the marketers of the credit card are very aware). In addition, many people use credit cards to build credit, which in turn is used to finance some of the larger purchases in life such as cars and houses.

So, because credit cards are such an integral part of our modern economic landscape, and will be a tool you'll have access to all throughout your adult life, we rank it as perhaps the second most important financial principle to understand at this stage of your life, right behind the principle of compounding interest.

Before we dig into the numbers, let's take a moment to define this financial tool.

What is a Credit Card, Anyway?

As you likely already know, a credit card allows you to instantly borrow money from a bank to buy things – a tank of gas, a ticket to a concert, a McDonald's cheeseburger, or a MacBook Pro.

As long as you pay back the money you borrow within the

"grace period" of 25-30 days after you monthly bill is issued, you don't have to pay extra for that loan.

But, if you don't pay your balance in full during those 25-30 days – something that the credit card company is counting on – you'll have to pay compounding interest on top of what you borrowed. And that interest can add up.

How much so? To illustrate, let's pretend *you're* a credit card company who's on the receiving end of all that sweet, sweet interest, and run through some of the numbers.

Let's imagine for a moment that you were to issue a credit card to your neighbors across the street so they could pay for a two-week, dream Caribbean cruise. After totaling all the airfare, hotel, tips, shore excursions, doggy daycare, and house-sitting expenses, your neighbors rack up a cool $10,000 on that credit card you issued.

They then return from the cruise with some new sunglasses and a bad sunburn, and now they start paying you back.

But they can't pay you back all at once. Like most of us, they can't just grab 10 large from out of an old coffee can buried in the back yard. They can only **pay you back $250 every month** (or about half the cost of an iPad). And because you're charging what all other credit card companies charge, your compounding interest rate is currently sitting at **19.49% APR** (we'll define APR in just a moment).

For the pleasure of going to the Bahamas for two weeks, your neighbors will now be giving you $250 per month – or about 6 new iPads per year – **for more than five years.**

Pretty sweet deal, huh? For you, that is.

Oh, and by the time the $10,000 is fully repaid, your neighbors will have also handed you **over $6,200** in interest on top of what they owed you in the first place – that's more than 10 iPads-worth of interest payments. That $10,000 trip just turned into a $16,200 trip.

Heck, the *mafia* doesn't make that much money on their loans.

(Well, we don't have any actual experience with the mafia outside of *Godfather* movies and *The Sopranos*, but we can't imagine them charging any more than that. Even the mafia needs to get repaid.)

Credit Cards and a Credit Score

To qualify for the credit cards that offer the lowest interest rates and the highest levels of rewards, you need to have good to excellent credit – you'll need to build and maintain a good credit score. So, even though we've mentioned how you'll be enticed with rewards such as travel miles or cash rebates, the highest levels of bonuses are often out of reach when we're just starting out, regardless of whether we're still in school or have just entered the workforce.

Herein lies the Catch-22 of credit, and thus the credit score.

If you don't *have* credit, it can be difficult to *get* credit.

So, for better or worse, if you have your sights set on making bigger purchases like a house, you often need to lay the groundwork by using credit cards responsibly at first to build your credit. (Later in this book, we will talk about some options for making bigger purchases without having to have much of a credit track record. As it happens, these are the options we prefer.)

Here are some options for building an excellent credit file.

Be a Deadbeat. Really, It's Okay.

You probably have heard the term "deadbeat" before, and if so, you probably know that being called a deadbeat is not exactly a compliment. In most instances, a deadbeat refers to someone who is unable to pay their bills, someone of low financial standing, or a potential customer not even worth wasting time pitching because of their inability to pay.

But when it comes to credit card usage, being called a deadbeat is the ultimate compliment. Credit card companies call some of their customers deadbeats when those customers pay off their balance every month, thus avoiding finance charges completely.

So when it comes to credit cards, be a deadbeat. Please!

If you're able to achieve deadbeat status – at least in the eyes of the credit card company – then credit cards can be a great tool to have in your financial utility belt. Deadbeats are able to effectively borrow money interest free, while at the same time racking up points for things like airplane tickets, hotel stays, gift cards, and a host of other rewards.

That brings us back to the Catch-22 of credit. It is much easier to say "pay your credit card in full every month" than it is to do. And according to recent data from the Federal Reserve, households in the U.S. are currently carrying about *four trillion dollars* of credit card debt[1] – proof positive that paying off a card in full is easier said than done.

Remember, the executives at credit card companies are playing a game, one which funnels millions of dollars into their own pockets. The object of the game is to make sure that you are <u>not</u> a deadbeat customer. Credit card company executives take two-week Caribbean cruises all the time, and they do it with the compound interest that all of their customers are paying them.

At this very moment, some credit card exec is planning their next Caribbean vacation – and they're planning on you paying for it.

Your job then, as someone who has been educated on these financial concepts, is not to let them win the game – and thus profit – at your expense.

CHAPTER FOUR

SUPPOSEDLY FUN THINGS THAT ARE REALLY, REALLY EXPENSIVE

We've put this chapter together using a three-act construct that's as old as time: the good news, followed by the bad news, followed once again by the good news.

Beginning, middle, end.

We'll use this construct to detail some of the principles and rules that can help you build substantial wealth during your lifetime, the systemic challenges you'll face as you build that wealth, and then finally how you can overcome those challenges, with the hopes of ultimately achieving whatever vision of financial success most resonates with you.

Naturally, the vision of financial success will differ widely from person to person. One individual might want to build a multi-million-dollar investment portfolio that will allow them to pursue ambitious travel goals, like seeing the Seven Wonders of the World. Another individual might want to use these same resources to pass an inheritance to kids or grandkids, or build a house of their dreams, or donate to their favorite charity, or endow a scholarship for talented cellists, or have a football stadium named after them (a la T. Boone Pickens, mentioned in Chapter 1) or some combination of all of the above.

For simple illustration purposes, this chapter is going to assume your lifetime savings goal is a bit more banal: you're going to save up to buy a $92,000 sports car for your 50th birthday, just in time for your mid-life crisis.

What if we told you that you could open an investment account this afternoon, contribute a portion of your work and/or allowance money into it while working summer and part-time jobs, and then save all you needed for that swaggy car by the time you were out of college?

How would that work, you ask?

There are no *absolute* guarantees in life or in the world of finance, but that's exactly what Meri and I will be showing you in this chapter. How it works. And how it works will involve the opposing forces of the Rule of 72 and inflation.

How it works is that you have to save money in investment accounts and resist the advertisements and peer pressure and marketing that you're bombarded with every day as you scroll through your social media feed.

Let's get to it.

The Rule of 72 – How Small Investments Become Big Dollars

Let's begin with a look at how money grows over time. In the previous chapter, we examined the principles of compounding interest, and the principle of paying yourself first. We looked at how relatively small investments each and every paycheck can add up significantly over time.

But just how much time?

One of the other most important financial concepts that can be learned – regardless of age – is a principle called the **Rule of 72.** Knowing about the Rule of 72 helps us answer that question of *how much time?*

Here's how it works: The Rule of 72 is a simple calculation that tells you *how many years it will take for your investments to <u>double</u> at a given interest rate.* The Rule's calculation says that you divide the interest rate, expressed as a percentage, into the number **72.**

That's it. That's the whole thing..

Divide interest rate by 72 and that's how long it takes to double your money.

So, let's use an example of 7.5 percent return (I'll show you how we can up with this number later in this chapter). If you have an investment that yields an average of 7.5 percent annually, it will take **10 years** for that money to double.

If you've just checked this on your iPhone, you'll notice that we're rounding the years up just a bit. To be more precise: 72 divided by 7.5 equals 9.6, so technically you can expect an investment with an annual rate of return of 7.5% will double in just *under* 10 years. We're estimating on the safe side here.

So, let's say that you are able to contribute $10,000 into an investment account by your 21st birthday. As we explored in the previous chapter, this amount is within reach for most whose parents cover some of the necessities like food, shelter, and perhaps car insurance costs. In any event, if you begin working when you're 16, and contribute an average of about 200 bucks a month in an indexed fund (we'll talk more about investments like index funds later on), you can expect to have roughly $10,000 set aside by that time. Again, this is a conservative estimate. If we return to the compound interest calculator introduced in the previous chapter and plug in the numbers, saving $200 a month at 7.5% interest means that we can estimate just over $11,500 in savings over a 4-year span.

*The Rule of 72 tells you how many years it will take for your investments to **double** at a given interest rate.*

If you just left that money alone, and the money grew at a rate of 7.5 percent per year, the Rule of 72 says that the $11.5k would become $23k at age 30, $46K at age 40, and $92k at age 50, and then $184k at age 60. You go down to the Ferrari dealership and write a check for $92,000 and drive off the lot as the proud owner, and you haven't saved a single nickel for that new Ferrari since you were mowing lawns in the summers of your youth. Not too shabby.

That's the Rule of 72 at work.

Why We Keep using the 7.5% Interest Rate

There's a reason why we've used 7.5% several times so far as an estimated rate of return on our invested money. It's because there just so happens to be an investment that averages a return of roughly 7.5% per year.

The United States stock market.

In fact, here's the one chart that I like to show clients more than any other chart about the U.S. stock market, or indeed about investing, period.

Annual Returns for the S&P 500 including dividends and excluding inflation:

Year	Return	Year	Return
2000	-9.11	2010	15.1
2001	-11.98	2011	2.1
2002	-22.27	2012	16.0
2003	28.72	2013	32.4
2004	10.82	2014	13.7
2005	4.79	2015	1.4
2006	15.74	2016	11.9
2007	5.46	2017	19.7
2008	-37.0	2018	-4.41
2009	26.5	2019	31.10

What does this chart say? It says that the market, over time, *wants* to return about 13.6% over the past 10 years and 5.9% over the past 20 years. For illustration purposes I elected to use 7.5 percent on your investments. It says that you can have a reasonable expectation – not a guarantee, of course, but an expectation – that when invested in U.S. stocks, your money will double about every 10 years.

And please don't miss the part of not adjusted for inflation. Inflation is another important financial concept which we'll cover in more detail in the following section. When we measure by the S&P

500 Index – an index that includes 500 of the United States' largest publicly-traded companies – and look all the way back to 1928, the average rate of return for US stocks is a very healthy 10 percent.[1]

Yeah, but 1928 is ancient history, you say. To which I say, *fair enough.* But if you slice the historical data in a less-favorable way that still accurately conveys long-term trends, and included the years 1950 to 2009, which was the year after the 2008 financial crash (a time period which also includes the 2001-2002 dot-com crash, and the oil/OPEC crashes of the 70s), *and adjust for inflation,* the return on investment over that 60 years is… almost 10%.[2]

Hellooo! 1950 is still not relevant, you say. *Dear old people: I'm more interested in 2050. My parents have told me about Bernie Madoff, and the housing crisis, and I've seen the* Wolf of Wall Street. *The stock market is just one big casino, and I'm not much into gambling, not that I have any money to gamble anyway, and not that it's even legal for me to gamble. Right now, I'm more worried if there's even going to be a stock market when 2050 finally rolls around. The stock market might fall into the ocean in another 30 years if climate trends continue.*

OK. Again fine, I say. We can't do much about the heating of our planet, but if it's any solace, let's just control what we can control. Let's just look at the U.S. stock market returns of *only* the twenty-year period between 2000 and 2019, a period we're choosing to make sure we factor in the nearly 40% drop in market value of 2008.

Here's how the S&P 500 did over those last ten years:

Year	Return	Year	Return
2000	-9.11	2010	15.1
2001	-11.98	2011	2.1
2002	-22.27	2012	16.0
2003	28.72	2013	32.4
2004	10.82	2014	13.7
2005	4.79	2015	1.4
2006	15.74	2016	11.9
2007	5.46	2017	19.7
2008	-37.0	2018	-4.41
2009	26.5	2019	31.10

When you add it all up, here's the result: Over the past 10 years, the stock market has returned 13.6% per year. (Even when adjusted for inflation, the annualized return is 8.57%.[3])

Now, then: how long do you plan on being around? Another 40 years? 60? 80? As you begin the very first steps of earning and saving your money, you should have this Rule of 72 firmly in your mind.

Knowing about the Rule of 72 will help you estimate how much your current savings will compound, *as long as that money is given plenty of time to grow.*

So if the Rule of 72 helps you understand how your money might double in 9.6 years, and might double again 9.6 years after that, there's another factor you must consider as you build this savings. It's the spending power of that doubled (or quadrupled) money will have once the day arrives when you actually go to spend it.

You may have noticed that things slowly tend to get more expensive over time. What you're noticing is a phenomenon known as *inflation.*

Inflation

Compound interest helps you build wealth. The Rule of 72 helps you estimate how long it will take that wealth to grow, and how much that wealth will be over a given period of time.

In the example we're using in this chapter, we're imagining a 30-year period for our money to grow. The inflation rate describes the actual spending power of that money 30 years from now.

To understand the basics of inflation, just ask yourself – or ask your parents – this simple question: generally speaking, are things *more* expensive today, or were they more expensive 30 years ago? Think big-ticket items. In terms of housing, are rent and mortgage payments more today, or 30 years ago? Are cars more expensive today, or 30 years ago? And what about salaries? Does the typical worker make more money today, or 30 years ago? (As a quick point of reference, the minimum wage 30 years ago was $4.25 per hour.[4])

This is more of a rhetorical question, of course. If yours truly ask your parents if the cost of a house is more today or 30 years ago, they likely to look at you as though you've been chasing parked cars.

Simply stated, **inflation** is the percent increase (or decrease) in prices during a specified period. Usually, inflation is expressed as an annual percentage rate, just like our returns on investment are expressed as an annual percentage rate. The stock market returns 10% annually. The average inflation rate is 2.5% annually.

To use another everyday example, let's look at the price of gasoline. If the inflation rate for a gallon of gas is 2 percent a year, then you can expect gas prices to be 2 percent higher next year. If a gallon of gas costs $3.00 this summer, then the price will be about $3.06 by the time you're ready for next summer's road trip.

Again, keep in mind that these things are expressed as *averages*. In the short term, there is almost no way to predict what gas will cost next summer. It could be $1 a gallon, it could be $6 a gallon. But over the course of 30 years, the inflation rate is much more predictable. Using a $3 gallon of gas as a starting point, and assuming a 2.5 percent inflation rate, we can reasonably assume that a gallon of gas will cost $6.30 per gallon by the time you're in your 50s.[5]

What Causes Inflation?

Even though it's a force that erodes the spending power of our dollar with each passing year, inflation isn't necessarily a terrible thing, just as money itself isn't a terrible thing. Money is essential for building the structures that provide shelter, for growing the plants and animals we require to eat, and the scientific advances that prolong our lives. In fact, inflation actually is a natural, inescapable byproduct of the modern credit-based economy. What we mean by "modern" in this context is the economic system that's been in place more or less since the 18th century, and what we mean by "credit-based" is a system that whereby a bank lends money so that people can build factories or open businesses with the belief that over time, the money will be paid back with interest.

In his book, *Sapiens: A Brief History of Humankind*, author Yuval Noah Harari uses a brief story to perfectly illustrate how the credit economy works, and in so doing, also perfectly explains why, over time, prices will continue to rise: because the future contains more money, and more stuff, than it did in the past. Why? Because when most money is created in a credit economy, it's created out of thin air. In this example, which, while fictional, is very much like the modern economy actually works today, 2 million *imaginary* dollars are created based on little more than the *hope* that 2 million *actual* dollars will appear sometime in the future.

"…LET'S IMAGINE A SIMPLE EXAMPLE.

Samuel Greedy, a shrewd financier, founds a bank in El Dorado, California. A. A. Stone, an up-and-coming contractor in El Dorado, finishes his first big job, receiving payment in cash to the tune of $1 million. He deposits this sum in Mr. Greedy's bank. The bank now has $1 million in capital.

In the meantime, Jane McDoughnut, an experienced but impecunious[6] El Dorado chef, thinks she sees a business opportunity — there's no really good bakery in her part of town. But she doesn't have enough money of her own to buy a proper facility complete with industrial ovens, sinks, knives and pots. She goes to the bank, presents her business plan to Greedy, and persuades him that it's a worthwhile investment. He issues her a $1 million loan, by crediting her account in the bank with that sum.

McDoughnut now hires Stone, the contractor, to build and furnish her bakery. His price is $1,000,000. When she pays him, with a check drawn on her account, Stone deposits it in his account in the Greedy bank. So how much money does Stone have in his bank account? Right, $2 million. How much money, cash, is actually located in the bank's safe? Yes, $1 million.

It doesn't stop there.

As contractors are wont to do, two months into the job Stone informs McDoughnut that, due to unforeseen problems and expenses, the bill for constructing the bakery will actually be $2 million. Mrs. McDoughnut is not pleased, but she can hardly stop the job in the middle. So, she pays another visit to the bank, convinces Mr. Greedy to give her an additional loan, and he puts another $1 million in her account. She transfers the money to the contractor's account.

How much money does Stone have in his account now? He's got $3 million.

But how much money is actually sitting in the bank? Still just $1 million. In fact, the same $1 million that's been in the bank all along."

AND THAT, YOUNG PEOPLE, IS HOW $2 MILLION IS INJECTED INTO A very small economy. Except what do people do once they know (or at least sense) that an extra $2 million is sitting around in people's bank accounts?

They charge more for their goods and services. To be precise, they charge about 2.5%, on average, every single year. For gallons of gas, for gallons of milk, as well as jeans, joggers, haircuts, happy meals, appliances, and automobiles.

But back to the story of how inflation impacts *your* life, and how it will mean that your current money won't be quite as valuable as your present money.

There are two primary drivers of inflation. The most common is what's known as **demand-pull** inflation. That's when demand outpaces supply for goods or services. Buyers want a product so much they are willing to pay higher prices. For example, a new iPhone 10 years ago cost around $500. Today they're around $1000.

Cost-push inflation is a second and less common cause. Cost push occurs when *supply* is restricted, but demand is not.

This occurs most often when there's some kind of natural disaster that impacts the ability to supply a commodity that's needed no matter the price. Recent hurricanes have presented some head-line-grabbing examples. Damaged gas supply lines affected supply, but people still needed to get to work and deliver truckloads of food to grocery stores. Demand remained constant for something that was suddenly restricted in supply, resulting in short-term spikes to the price of gasoline.

And as we have just seen in the previous anecdote, many experts say that an ever-increasing money supply also causes inflation. There is still some healthy debate about how much this is actually the case (Meri and I both agree with the concept, by the way), but in general the theory posits that inflation's primary cause is the printing of money by world governments – which these govern-ments do by selling bonds. In any event, the extra money then chases a limited set of goods, which in turn creates inflation by trig-gering either demand-pull or cost-push inflationary events.

In the chapter that follows, we'll talk in more detail about the very printing of money when we discuss the concept (yes, it's a concept) of cash.

Inflation and the CPI

One of the terms you may hear about occasionally that's synony-mous with inflation is something known as the Consumer Price Index, or the CPI.

The U.S. Bureau of Labor Statistics calculates the CPI by gath-ering information from 23,000 businesses, and 80,000 consumer items[7]. The government also factors in sales taxes and even the monthly cost of owning or renting a home.

In short, the CPI turns an abstract discussion of inflation into a number that everyone can then reference to make decisions. The most significant decision-making entity in this regard is the Federal Reserve Bank (the Fed), which uses the CPI to set interest rates on the money it loans out in the form of Treasury Bills. This has cascading effects in other areas of the economy, affecting everything from home loans to stock market returns and more. By dialing the rate of Treasury Bills up and down, the Fed generally aims to keep inflation at a "sweet spot" of about 2-3 percent. The governors of the Fed want people to keep opening new bakeries and buying things like new baking ovens with borrowed money, but they also don't want inflation to get so high that it causes manufacturers to cut back because raw materials cost so much – the baker won't make as many muffins if buying the muffin flour costs twice as much as it did a few months ago.

The CPI is updated every month, so curious souls can always get the latest info about the rate of inflation. For example, at the time of this writing, the annual CPI for the year ending May 2019 was 1.9%, which is a tad lower than historical averages. That means that from May 2018 to May 2019, the cost of everything you need to get through your month – from toothpaste to toilet paper to tomatoes – cost 1.9 percent more than it did a year ago.

--

Let's wrap up our discussion of inflation by returning to the example of the fancy sports car you're planning to buy for your 50th birthday. If you have your eye on an $80,000 car today, you already know how much you'll need to save up by your 21st birthday ($10,000), and how long it will take for that $10,000 to become $80,000.

It would be wise for you to figure how much that potential car might be when you go car shopping again in 30 years. If we plug the numbers into the compound interest calculator on moneychimp.com, you'll see that in 30 years, that $80,000 car might be priced at $167,000 because of the inflationary pressures on the price of cars.

So if inflation is one of the obstacles to plan for when saving and investing your hard earned dollars, what else do we need to be wary of when making longer-term plans?

Feeling Pressured to Buy Stuff

I'm sure you've heard of the phrase, "Keeping up with the Joneses."

No, I'm not talking about the 2017 comedy with Gal Gadot and Jon Hamm by the same name. I'm talking about an English idiom that refers to the way humans often compare themselves to their peers or neighbors, using that comparison as a benchmark for social class or the accumulation of material goods. If *they* get the newest iPhone, *you* feel compelled to get a new iPhone. If *they* roll a brand-new car into the driveway, *you* don't want them to be the only ones with a sweet new ride.

In short, it's peer pressure.

To fail to "keep up with the Joneses" is to feel as though you have a lesser socio-economic standing than your peers.

The phrase originated in a 1913 comic strip that tracked the daily travails of the McGinis family and their desperate, flailing attempts to match the lavish lifestyle of their unseen neighbors, the Joneses.

I've mentioned the Kardashians before, and should here once again, as that show tries to convince you to... flail about in a desperate attempt to match their lavish lifestyle. If you're a fan of that show, that's perfectly fine. Just be a fan knowing that the Kardashians are being paid millions and millions of dollars to try to get you... yeah. They want you to buy stuff that people who don't have a television show can't afford.

Resisting the urge to keep up with the Joneses is *much* easier said than done. That's because there are two social forces at work here. One is the credit economy, which as mentioned, allows us to buy things today in the hope that we'll make more money in the future. The other is the modern cultural ways in which we demonstrate status.

Social standing once depended greatly on one's family name — and to a large extent, it still does. However, the rise of global consumerism beginning shortly after the Industrial Revolution gave rise to increased social mobility.

For example, the caste system of many Hindu countries is no

longer officially in place, any more than the nobility and peasant social strata of pre-Enlightenment Europe. With the increasing availability of things to buy, we therefore have become more and more inclined to define ourselves by our possessions. We don't have colorful feathers to display like birds trying to attract a life partner, so many of us go about impressing our friends and potential romantic companions with things like fashionable clothes, big houses, hot tubs, leather-bound books, tickets to the Fyre festival, or a rare sneaker collection.

And then we Instagram about it.

But this is nothing new. Conspicuous consumption and materialism have been a driving force of human behavior for many hundreds of years. Grown men in 17th century Europe wore frilly wigs and robes to show off their wealth, and then a few years later people seemed to come to the collective realization that… *Oh, those are just wigs. Kinda stupid when you think about it.* Likewise, grown men in 20th century America wear Rolexes to show off their wealth, and someday soon, we'll collectively look back and realize… *Oh, those just tell time.*

But the larger point is that neither the credit economy nor consumerism are necessarily bad things. In our view, it's actually a sign of cultural progress that our social status isn't defined solely because of the family we were born into. But the thing to remember about seeing the material things that others have is simply this:

Looks can be deceiving.

Let's go back to the example of the car. Many adults who drive around the suburbs in their giant SUVs, or even many kids pulling into high school in a 2-year-old Mercedes, all while posting selfies on new cell phones, are *deeply* in debt.

And as we've discussed, most debt is bad. Debt is compounding interest working *against* you, when the objective for most of personal finance – really the way I spend more of my professional life – is trying to get compounding interest working in favor of my clients.

Now, if you ask these same kids or adults how they are doing, they'll say they are fine. They will tell you they made their last car and credit card payments, and that you're being a killjoy just for asking in the first place. And yet according to a recent Federal Reserve Board study, 43% of American families spend more than they earn.

So how can you combat the desire to keep up with the Joneses?

Fortunately, one of the keys lies with something we discussed very early on in this book. The best weapon in your fight against the peer pressure to buy stuff is to have a clear understanding of your *priorities*.

And you thought we had you define a goal just for the fun of it.

Define Your Priorities

Ever done a yoga class? If you have, you're probably familiar with the habit of setting an *intention* for your day's practice. It's just a few seconds of reflection where you stop and consider the questions of "Why am I here?" and "What do I want to get out of this stretchy, sweaty routine in the first place?" In a yoga class, your intention can simply be to get flexible, or get stronger, or just spend an hour not thinking about anything besides the next pose. (Not letting the mind wander is something that takes much more effort than you might think.)

When it comes to spending and saving and keeping up with the Joneses, we've found that a similar approach can work wonders. Once a day, or once a week, it can be very helpful to ask yourself questions like, "What's important to me right now? And "What am I spending all this time working and getting paid for, anyway?"

Once you clearly define your priorities, it becomes much more clear which things are deserving of your time and your money, and which things are not. Notice here that we're not using the word "need," as that concept gets overused. On one hand you don't need a cell phone at all. But on the other hand, you do need a cell phone so you can communicate with your parents, your teachers, and your employers. The questions isn't "Do you need *a* cell phone?" instead, the question is "Do you need *this* cell phone?"

The bottom line is that when you are planning for your future, you need to carefully monitor the things that take up your time and your income today.

It's your money and your life, so spend both of these wisely.

Keeping Up with the Joneses Can (Sometimes) Be Good

There's a flip side of the "keeping up with the Joneses" behavior that can prove very beneficial to our personal financial standing. It happens when you align yourself with like-minded peers, who are also working and saving so they can attend college, or so they can pay cash for a really nice car once they hit age 50.

Associating yourself with others who are also setting their own financial goals can often result in a cognitive bias known as "anchoring." Anchoring happens when you or I latch onto the first number or price point we hear, and then view that as the "normal" price for something.

For example, is a $50 workout shirt a good deal? I would argue that no, it's not – that you can find perfectly good workout shirts for much less than $50. But if I walk into a store where most of the workout shirts are selling for $90 (cough, Lululemon, cough), the "anchor point" for shirts has been set at $90. When you see the $50 one on the clearance rack, you don't think, *Damn! Who pays $50 for shirt?* Instead, you're much more likely to think, *Holy cow! I just found a great deal on this shirt!*

Put into more personal financial terms: If you have a close friend who is setting aside $150 per month toward their college expenses, the anchor point for monthly college savings has been set at $150. Are you going to match your friend's contribution? Or are you going to try to top that contribution by striving to making yours $175?

You're good friends and all, but you can do better than $150, right? Right?

Right.

The big takeaway here is to surround yourself with people whose money habits you'd like to emulate. Those people will help set the anchor points against which you'll measure your standing among that group of peers. Once you do that, you won't feel as conflicted between your desire to save and your desire to please your friends, since doing those two things will be in alignment.

You may have even noticed a bit of subtle anchoring that Meri and I have deployed earlier in this chapter. The amount of that anchor was $200 a month, and $10,000 by the time of your 21st birthday.

But you can beat that mark, right?

Right?

CHAPTER FIVE

FINANCIAL STUFF YOU'LL USE EVERY DAY

The Story Of Money

Think about what's in your pocket right now. Whether money is a slip of paper with some words and faces printed on it, or a round coin stamped with a bird, a bear, or maybe a bell, along with the date in which the coin was minted, or it's a series of ones and zeroes stored digitally on your smart phone, everyone reading this right now has at least *some* amount of money within easy reach.

But what exactly is money, anyway?

As it turns out, this is an incredibly interesting question. And as most of us spend the vast majority of our waking hours in pursuit of money – yes, we might be in a rock band and truly love what we do and not really care whether or not we get paid, but until humans figure out a way to survive without calories, even those playing in a rock band (or producing EDM) must eventually figure out a way to get people to pay for either tickets or downloads – it's also a question worthy of our consideration.

If you have a coin or dollar bill in your pocket, it might have been *issued* (i.e. created) by a particular government entity like the

U.S. Department of the Treasury, or the Mexican Central Bank. Does that make it money?

You might also notice that your coin or paper slip includes some appeal to a mythical being. But coins and paper slips throughout the world also have invocations to different mythical beings.[1] So does religious symbolism suddenly turn a round piece of metal into money?

And if we have the misfortune to end up in jail because we've been framed for a crime we didn't commit? Or stranded on a remote island that doesn't have a central bank? Can cigarettes be money? Can seashells?

In both cases, the answer is yes.

The bottom line is that cash is whatever a collection of human beings *believe* is cash.

CASH HAS BEEN NECESSARY FOR HUMAN COMMERCE BECAUSE EVER since the Agricultural Revolution, the exchange of goods and services amongst humans has become overwhelmingly complex – a barter system was just not possible once humans stopped organizing themselves in hunter-gatherer communities. After all, hunter-gatherer communities had no need for money. They created everything they required to live through a system of exchanging favors and obligations. If I was a hunter, I would share some of the meat from the recent sabretooth tiger hunt in exchange for some medicine from the community elders to soothe aching muscles or patch up missing chunks of flesh – sabretooths don't go down without a fight, as it turns out.

But this system starts breaking down once we start growing plants (and livestock for that matter) full time. Once we cross that threshold, we need cash.

How so? Let's look at a quick example. As in the previous chapter, the book *Sapiens* provides a fantastic illustration of how money is required when people begin to specialize – when one person concentrates on growing grain, while another concentrates on teaching linguistics, while yet another develops and sells their skills as a writer.

Once we began specializing, and then began moving ever closer to other professionals, we had to come up with something better.

"Densely populated cities provided full-time employment not just for profes-sional shoemakers and doctors, but also for carpenters, priests, soldiers and lawyers. Villages that gained a reputation for producing really good wine, olive oil or ceramics discovered that it was worth their while to specialize nearly exclu-sively in that product and trade it with other settlements for all the other goods they needed. This made a lot of sense. Climates and soils differ, so why drink mediocre wine from your backyard if you can buy a smoother variety from a place whose soil and climate is much better suited to grape vines?... But specialization created a problem – how do you manage the exchange of goods between the specialists?

Imagine that you own an apple orchard in the hill country that produces the crispest, sweetest apples in the entire province. You work so hard in your orchard that your shoes wear out. So you harness up your donkey cart and head to the market town down by the river. Your neighbor told you that a shoemaker on the south end of the marketplace made him a really sturdy pair of boots that's lasted him through five seasons. You find the shoemaker's shop and offer to barter some of your apples in exchange for the shoes you need. The shoemaker hesitates. How many apples should he ask for in payment? Every day he encounters dozens of customers, a few of whom bring along sacks of apples, while others carry wheat, goats or cloth – all of varying quality. Still others offer their expertise in peti-tioning the king or curing backaches. The last time the shoemaker exchanged shoes for apples was three months ago, and back then he asked for three sacks of apples. Or was it four? But come to think of it, those apples were sour valley apples, rather than prime hill apples. On the other hand, on that previous occa-sion, the apples were given in exchange for small women's shoes. This fellow is asking for man-size boots. Besides, in recent weeks a disease has decimated the flocks around town, and skins are becoming scarce. The tanners are starting to demand twice as many finished shoes in exchange for the same quantity of leather. Shouldn't that be taken into consideration? In a barter economy, every day the shoemaker and the apple grower will have to learn anew the relative prices of dozens of commodities. If one hundred different commodities are traded in the market, then buyers and sellers will have to know 4,950 different exchange rates.

... It gets worse. Even if you manage to calculate how many apples equal one pair of shoes, barter is not always possible. After all, a trade requires that each side want what the other has to offer. What happens if the shoemaker doesn't like apples and, if at the moment in question, what he really wants is a divorce? True, the farmer could look for a lawyer who likes apples and set up a three-way deal. But what if the lawyer is full up on apples but really needs a haircut?"

The answer to all these questions for most societies since the dawn of the Agricultural Revolution has been to create a system of connecting large numbers of experts.

That system is known as money.

Using Cash

Cash is legal *tender* – currency or coins – that can be used to exchange goods, debt or services.

Now: cool marbles or Pokémon cards can *also* be used to pay for goods or services, but these aren't *legal* tender, meaning that marbles and Pokémon cards, as valuable as they might be to some, can't be used to settle a dispute in a court of law. Someone can't hire you to mow their lawn for $20, and then give you a sack of marbles as payment, even if the person offering the sack of marbles claims the marbles are really worth $50. Were the dispute to end up in a court-room, the judge would enter an order for payment in legal tender, or cash. (On the other hand, if you were to have emailed the person and had agreed to accept marbles as payment, and the person would be able to enter the email as evidence, the judge might make a different finding.)

In any event, we here in the United States have Spain – and

more specifically Spain's colonization efforts in the Americas during the middle of the previous millennia – to thank for the cash dollars we keep in our pockets today. Virtually *all* cash used in North and South America is based on the Spanish dollar, which were also known as a **piece of eight**, or the **peso**. The Spanish dollar was a silver coin which was worth eight Spanish *reales*. (Simply put, the value of a single Spanish dollar could be divided into 8 units, much like a U.S. dollar can be divided into four quarters, or ten 10ths, and so on.)

The Spanish dollar even remained legal *tender* (there's that word again) in the United Stated – it could be used to pay for rum, or shoes, or tickets to a stage play – until the Coinage Act of 1857. Because it was widely used throughout the world, the Spanish dollar became the first world currency by the late 18th century. The Canadian dollar, Japanese yen, Chinese yuan, Philippine peso, and several currencies were initially based on the Spanish dollar.

So even though we've been using cash for several hundred years, using it to pay for things today feels almost as antiquated as the Spanish piece of eight coin itself. Meri and I probably use cash more often than younger generations do, but even still, there are days and sometimes even weeks when we don't use cash to pay for a single thing. Whether it be gas, groceries, or lunch at the food truck which parks a few blocks away from Meri's school, we've become quite used to the convenience of swiping and going on with our day.

In terms of how modern consumers and businesses think of cash, the word can also be used to indicate money sitting in banking accounts, checks, or any other form of currency that is easily accessible *and can be quickly turned into physical cash.* If I write you a check for $100, for example, you could immediately exchange that check for physical cash at either your bank or mine.

Thus, in a modern economy, cash also refers to the string of ones and zeroes in our bank accounts that can be instantly accessed by using another string of ones and zeroes that's stored either on the magnetic stripe of a card, or a chip embedded in a card, or a unique string of ones and zeroes that's stored on an individual's smart phone.

Cash in its physical form is the simplest, most broadly accepted and reliable form of payment, which is why many businesses only accept cash. Why physical cash? Because checks can bounce. Credit cards can be declined. If you've ever tried to pay for something at an outdoor event like a music festival in the desert, or at a business whose Internet connection is down, you might have first-hand experience with the fact that even debit card transactions require a signal to work. Plus, there's a cost to the vendor for the processing of a credit transaction, so some merchants don't even accept credit, or don't accept certain forms of credit – they'll accept Visa, but not American Express, for example.

However, cash requires no extra processing. (In terms of the cash a debit card makes available, it's a complex and almost magical process that involves electronic handshakes between several financial institutions. Unlike with a credit card transaction, in the end a debit card transaction *immediately* transfers money from one account to another once the transaction is approved. This is why debit cards are considered equivalent to cash by almost every business. As long as they have a signal, that is.)

That said, there are some significant *disadvantages* to doing business in cash, the largest of which may be the issue of tracking and accounting for it. Sometimes, this issue is known as "employee theft," an issue which is otherwise known as "shrinkage." In too many businesses, cash goes missing, and it's not because it gets stolen by criminals wearing clown masks.

Sometimes when we're out adulting, we want to buy things that we don't necessarily have the cash for. These things can include large purchases like houses, automobiles, or a year at the university. All too often, they include smaller purchases like iPhones or steak dinners.

No matter the size of the purchase, when we're spending money that we don't immediately have on hand, we're asking someone for a *loan*.

Getting a Loan

Simply stated, a loan is a *contract* between two individuals, two businesses, or between an individual and a business. The contract specifies the amount loaned, the repayment schedule, and, in most cases, the purpose of the loan.

Why the purpose of the loan? Businesses who might loan you money for a new home or car want that money spent on homes or cars. If you take out a car loan and then spend the money on a trip to Peru to take selfies at Machu Picchu, you're statistically less likely to pay back that loan – the bank can repossess the car; they won't get quite as much value out of your cool llama selfies. Oh, and you will have also committed fraud in the process, something for which you can be prosecuted and perhaps sent to jail. But hey… on the bright side, you'll get to use cigarettes as money.

In some cases, though, you can use loans for whatever you want. For example, a very common type of loan adults use is a *home equity* loan, which is an open-ended line of credit, up to a specified limit, which can be used for renovating the kitchen, paying for college, or yes… even a trip to Machu Picchu. A home equity loan doesn't require you to specify the loan's purpose.

Meanwhile, the *terms* of a loan are agreed to by each party in the transaction before any money or property changes hands. Often with large loans, the lender requires *collateral*. Collateral is a legal right to take possession of something in the event that the loan terms are broken, and if collateral is required to secure the loan, this will be spelled out in the loan documents.

In fact, your first credit card may be a *secured* credit card, which is a credit card whose collateral is a deposit at the bank that issued the credit card. In most cases, having a secured credit card means you're unable to get your hands on your deposit unless the balance of the secured credit card is zero. In the event you don't pay the card, the bank simply extracts the money needed to pay off the account from your deposit.

Finally, most loans will include provisions regarding the maximum amount of interest, as well as other language outlining the length of time before repayment is required. In the case of a student loan, it's often the case that payments on the loan are deferred until you're out of college and employed, and thus have the means to repay the loan.

Throughout the book, we will be discussing specific types of loans, and their possible impact on your life. In particular, we'll be focusing on three large loans that will likely be most relevant for the late teen and early adult:

- **The student loan** – used to fund an education.
- **The car loan** – used to purchase a car.
- **The mortgage** – used to buy a house.

Simple vs. Compound Interest

The interest rate on loans can be either *simple* interest or *compound* interest.

Simple interest is interest on the principal loan. For instance, if someone takes out a $100,000 student loan, and the loan agreement stipulates that the interest rate on the loan is 15%, this means that the borrower will have to pay back the original loan amount of $100,000 x 1.15 = $115,000.

By the way, banks never do this.

We've been over the principal of compound interest. We've been over the fact that bankers are quite aware of the wealth-building properties of compound interest. And so, guess what bankers work into the language of the loans they make?

Simple interest.

Kidding! *Of course* banks charge compound interest. As long as it's legal to do so, banks will *always* charge compound interest.

As you saw previously, compound interest is interest on top of interest. Compound interest means more interest payments by you, and more profits to the lender. The interest is not only applied on the principal, but also on accumulated interest of previous periods.

When you're dealing with particularly large loans, you might even hear the word accrued interest used. What's being described here how the banks are calculating interest. Here's how it works:

Let's say that you take out a $200,000 loan for your med school education. The interest rate on that loan is a modest 5%, and has a term of 10 years.

Does that mean that you'll only pay back $210,000 in the 10 years after you're done with school? Did you just come up with that number by multiplying $200,000 by .05 and get $10,000?

If you're nodding your head yes, then you've just <u>failed</u> today's lesson.

Pay attention!! Banks charge <u>compound</u> interest on loans, first because they can, and second because it makes them a *ton* more money. If you become a banker someday, you'll do the same.

If you borrow $200,000 at 5% and pay it back over 10 years, you'll end being charged **over $54,000** in compound interest.

How does that work?

Well, all of your post-med school monthly payments will be exactly $2121.31.[2] Your first payment will be used to retire $1287.98 of principal, and $833.33 interest. From the bank's perspective, the first month's payment is effectively a loan of $1287.98 for 10 years. If they were to take that same $1287.98 and invest it into something that paid 5% interest, they would make $833.33 if they just left it alone for 10 years.

Fair? Maybe, maybe not. How the game is played? Absolutely.

And understanding how loans work just helps us make better decisions about whether or not to take on a loan in the first place.

Please note that in most cases, large loans such as a loan for a house, or a loan for med school, represents a very good investment. If a $200,000 loan helps you obtain a mentally rewarding medical career that pays you $200,000 per year, then investing in med school is a tremendously profitable endeavor.

In this hypothetical, you'll make $2 million in salary over the 10 years after med school. After paying back the compounded loan, that'll net you roughly $1.75 million in 10 years, and many times more than that over an entire medical career, which should be plenty of money to cover other life necessities such as houses, cars, and college savings for your own kids.

Or, maybe even a trip to Machu Picchu.

Loans and Your Credit Score

It's hard to discuss loans without also incorporating a mention of the **credit score.**

Generally speaking, the credit score is the "grade" which will determine whether or not a lender approves you for a loan. And just like with final exams or the SAT, the higher the number, the better your grade.

There are several different companies like Experian and Transunion which keep track of your credit usage and provide a score on your creditworthiness, but the most significant of these – and the one that other companies use as a model – is something known as the **FICO score.**

Your FICO score will be maintained by the Fair Isaac Corporation (FI CO, get it?), and will be a number between 300 to 850. The higher the number, the more likely you are to repay your debts in the eyes of lenders. In general, scores above 650 indicate a very good credit history. On the other hand, if you have a score below 620, it can be difficult to obtain financing, or at least obtain financing at low interest rates.

Your FICO score takes these factors into consideration:

Payment history. Payment history refers to whether an individual pays his credit accounts on time. Credit reports show the payments submitted for each line of credit, and the reports indicate if the payments were received 30, 60, 90, 120 or more days late.

Total amount owed. Having a lot of debt does not necessarily equate to low credit scores. Rather, FICO considers the *ratio* of money owed to the amount of credit available. For example, an individual who owes $5,000 but has maxed out all his credit cards will likely have a lower credit score than an individual who owes $50,000 but is not close to the limit on any of his accounts. (And yes, some people have credit cards with six- or seven-figure credit limits.)

Length of credit history. As a general rule, the longer an individual has had credit, the better the score. However, with favorable scores in the other categories, even someone with a short credit history can have a good score. FICO takes into account how long the oldest account has been open, the age of the newest account, and the overall average.

Types of credit. In terms of credit scores, FICO sees it as favorable to have a mix of retail accounts, credit cards, installment loans such as vehicle loans, and mortgages.

New credit acquired. New credit refers to recently opened accounts. If the borrower has opened a bunch of new accounts in a short period of time, that indicates credit risk (i.e. why are you suddenly borrowing so much money?), and thus lowers the credit score.

Finally, bear in mind that the FICO score is just one factor – albeit a significant one – that determines whether or not you will be approved for a loan. Before making a decision about whether or not to fund a loan, lenders will also factor in other details such as income, how long the borrower has been at his job, and type of credit requested. If you have an 800 credit score (which is excellent) and try to take out a $250,000 home loan, but only make $12,000 per year bagging groceries part-time, it's *highly* unlikely that you'll be approved for the loan. (Maybe if you just got an inheritance and were making a $200,000 down payment you could pull it off, but that's really the only plausible scenario here.) For things like mortgages, you have to demonstrate both that you're creditworthy and have the *means* to repay the loan.

In this section covering loans, we've mentioned an annual salary of $200,000 several times.

But we'd also like to mention that you don't necessarily *have* to go to med school to make $200,000 a year.

Plenty of electricians, plumbers, roofers, mechanics, chefs, and a host of other craftsmen make this much and more (usually they have a few others working for them when this is the case, though). But whether you find yourself going on to make $200,000 a year, $20,000 a year, or $2 million a year, you'll also have to pay *taxes* on some of that income. It's another financial reality encountered every day, so it's another subject where a little understanding can provide significant advantages when compared to some in the general public.

Income tax

Along with "keeping up with the Joneses," you may have also heard the idiom "there are only two certainties in life: death and taxes." And it's true. Unless you are somehow able to survive this life without making any income, taxes will be an inescapable aspect of your financial existence.

Now, before we even begin this topic, know that we're <u>not</u> here to dissect political implications of taxation – how much is collected, the method of collection, and what the money is spent on. People spend their entire lives debating this issue. Suffice it to say that it's our view that modern societies couldn't really function without tax revenues, and that the enforcement of tax collection is one of the defining features of a nation. If the United States was suddenly unable to collect taxes, the country would cease to exist. (If you're a *Rick and Morty* fan, there's a darkly funny sequence that encapsulates this whole nations-stop-functioning-without-taxes-thing we're describing in about 10 seconds much better than anything we could write in a paragraph. Just do a quick search for "Rick and Morty: Rick Collapses the Galactic Government" on YouTube and you'll see what we mean.)

Currently, the U.S., along with most all other nations on the planet, utilize a **progressive** taxation system. A progressive tax refers to charging a higher tax rate for people who earn a higher income. In theory, the higher the income, the more you can afford to contribute to the collective well-being of your community, your state, or your country in the form of taxes. The rationale is that progressive taxation is more equitable: people with a lower income usually spend a greater percentage of their income just to maintain a basic standard of living. That is, relatively speaking, someone making $30,000 a year and someone making $300,000 a year spend roughly the same on basic necessities such as gallons of milk and gallons of gasoline. They both use the same highways to get to work or go on vacation. They both enjoy the protections of the military and police. A progressive tax system, then, asks the person making $300,000 a year to pay more in taxes mostly because *they can afford it.*

In any event, our job here is just simply to draw your attention to the taxes that you'll pay while you're out there working in your first jobs, which will probably pay you much less than $300,000. In addition, we'll briefly touch on the responsibilities associated with paying taxes to both federal and state governments.

We'll start here: an **income tax** is a tax that governments impose on income generated by businesses and individuals within their jurisdiction. By law, taxpayers must file an income tax return annually to determine their tax obligations.

In the United States, said tax return is filed with the Internal Revenue Service (IRS), which collects taxes and enforces tax law. The IRS employs a complex set of rules and regulations regarding reportable and taxable income, deductions, and credits. The agency collects taxes on all forms of income, such as wages, investments, and business earnings.

In its essence, an income tax return is a ledger that formally says something like this: *hey, government, here's all the money I earned, here are some things that can reduce my tax bill, and so here's the bottom line of what I owe in taxes. Also, here's what I've already paid in the form of payroll deductions.* (More about payroll deduction in just a bit.) If the amount owed in taxes is less than what you've already paid, then you get a tax refund. Sometimes however, you can do these same calculations and wind up with a tax liability. This is uncommon for most teens and early adults who receive a regular paycheck for things like bagging groceries or waiting tables, but tax liabilities aren't all that uncommon for people who are *self-employed*, like web designers or small business owners.

So… What About that Tax Return Thing?

We know what you might be thinking: *Look, man, I wanna work, and I also don't want to end up in trouble with the IRS. So was I supposed to file a tax return last year, or what?*

As we draft this in 2019,[3] we can pass along the info that was applicable to the tax year 2018. For that year, the requirements to file a tax return were that dependents *must* complete a tax return if their unearned income was over $1,050, or their earned income was over $12,000, or their gross income (earned and unearned income combined) was more than the larger of $1,050 or their earned income (up to $11,650) plus $350.

It's just that simple.

Let's now try to unpack this taxation thing just a bit further.

For starters, what exactly is **earned** income? According to the Internal Revenue Service, earned income is money you receive from *working* for someone who pays you, or income you receive from running a business or farm.

So, if you work in a grocery store, are you making earned income? Indeed you are.

Unearned income is income derived from investments and other sources which is unrelated to employment. Examples include interest from savings accounts, bond interest, alimony, and dividends from stock.

So, are you divorced, or do you have a large stock portfolio? Probably not, so you don't have any unearned income to report.

The Important Part – if You Want to Keep Money You've Made

The single most important part of taxation for the majority of teenagers and young adults who are working part time are as follows:

1. Teens almost always pay taxes in the form of payroll taxes.
2. Teens are required to file a tax return if their *earned* income is over $12,000.
3. Teens are required to file a tax return if their *unearned* income is over $1,050.
4. Teens almost always owe <u>zero</u> in federal taxes, and are almost always <u>owed a tax refund</u> by the IRS.
5. Teens can get back the money they've paid in federal taxes by filing a 1040EZ, which should take all of 15 minutes to file. *For many teens working part time, filing a 1040EZ will be the equivalent of working for $1000 an hour,* if not more.

So if you've made less than $12,000 in the last year through part-time work, then file a tax return! Get that money back! It's your money! Not only is filing a tax return a great exercise in adulting, but it's profitable, too. You recall that money goal we started talking about way back in Chapter 1? You might have made that amount already, and all that remains for you to do is file a 1040EZ.

Earned Income and the W-2

Oh, and how are you supposed to keep track of what you've made and what you've paid in payroll taxes while bagging groceries?

The good news is that you don't have to. Your employer is required to send you something called a **W-2 form** at the beginning of the year for the previous year's work. (The deadline for employers is January 31) Here's what the W-2 looks like:

As you can see, the W-2 consists of several boxes that report various items relating to your income. In box 1 of the W-2, you'll find your annual wage and salary payments. In box 2, you'll see the amount of federal tax withheld. This is probably the most important box for a teen working part time.

Why? Because **this is the amount you should receive back** when filing your return.

Once you receive your W-2 (or multiple W-2s) by about the first week in February, just use the numbers on the W-2 to file the one-page 1040EZ. Sign the 1040EZ, attach a copy of any form W-2s provided by your employer(s), and the IRS will process the refund. It can all be done electronically, and in most cases the money will be transferred into your account in a matter of days.

Paying that FICA Guy

As mentioned, when you work for someone, that someone is required to *withhold* (i.e. pay) federal taxes on your behalf. They do this as they are running payroll. The amount withheld in payroll taxes is based on the wage or salary of the employee.

There are some payroll taxes you can receive back when you file a tax return, as we have just discussed. There are other taxes that you cannot. In the United States, there are **three** primary line items that are deducted from paychecks:

- Federal Income taxes
- State Income taxes (in most states, that is)

- Social Security, and
- Medicare

We'll touch on these last two items here. Just who is that FICA guy, anyway?

Social Security and Medicare are funded by Federal Insurance Contributions Act (FICA) tax. The basic premise of Social Security and Medicare is that you pay into them while you are working. Later, upon retirement age (currently the government considers you at "full" retirement when you hit age 67), or under certain circumstances such as a permanent disability, you qualify to withdraw from those funds.

As with federal income taxes, the amount of your FICA payment will depend on your income. The higher the income, the higher your FICA payment. For Social Security contributions, there's a maximum wage base – no further Social Security contributions are made once you surpass wages of $132,900. There is no wage base limit for Medicare.

Because most teens don't make over $132k, they'll be paying 6.2% of their paychecks to Social Security, and 1.45% to Medicare. (Meanwhile, the employer pays taxes equal to the amounts withheld from employee earnings.)

Do you write code or make websites for people in your spare time? If so, good for you! You're probably making some good money renting out your computer skills.

But also if so, the law says that you have to pay taxes on that income. Self-employed individuals pay 12.4% in Social Security tax and 1.45% in Medicare tax. It's therefore not uncommon for independent-contractor types to have end-of-year tax bills they simply aren't prepared to pay.

The bottom line is that if you're writing code or developing websites in your spare time, *please* talk to a tax professional, or at least talk to your parents about talking to a tax professional. Ask for help. Having a large unpaid tax liability is a stupid reason that smart people find themselves in, and unfortunately this happens all the time. A good tax pro should be able to tell you how much to pay and where to pay in just a few minutes.

Finally, know that when it comes to Social Security and Medicare taxes (the FICA guy), you *don't* get that money back when you file your annual tax return.[4]

CHAPTER SIX

GETTING FROM A TO B. LITERALLY.

You Need a Car. Or Do You?

So, you need to buy a car to get from Point A to Point B.

After all, you need it to get to work. To school. To the mall. To the grocery store. To the movie theater. To the football game.

Now in fairness, you might *not* need a car, either. You may be able to do all the things we just mentioned with a good public transit system, a pair of walking shoes, and maybe a decent bicycle. But that's not what this chapter is about. And that doesn't mean that you won't need/want to buy a car at some point in the future.

If the geographic realities of your life require you to cover distances of several miles when going between activities (i.e. if you live in most suburban and rural areas of the U.S.), there comes a time when your parents can't haul you around in the minivan any longer, so you're gonna need to get your own car.

And when that time arrives, you're faced with essentially three options:

1. Have your parents buy you a car.
2. Go out and buy a car yourself.
3. Do some combination of both.

Let's look a little more carefully at the implications of each.

Parents Buy the Car

Of course, this isn't an option for everyone, but some parents are in the financial position to be able to simply buy a car for their teen, and sometimes even a shiny new one at that.

Now, according to Kelly Blue Book data, the average price of a light vehicle – a category which includes passenger cars and many pickup trucks – in the United States as of March 2019 was *over $36,000*. So, a few quick questions for parents who are considering getting Chet[1] a new Jeep or something for his 16th birthday: Is buying that new car about your teen, or about you? Are you trying to model the fiscal responsibility you'd like to see in your kids, or are you trying to be "cool?" Because Chet still won't think you're cool. What's more, Chet won't have any notion of how difficult it is to save $36,000, or what it means to take on the obligation of a $36,000 loan.

In short, buying a $36,000 car for a 16-year-old doesn't make sense.

If your parents have decided to buy you a car, then we invite you to have a conversation about what kind of car makes the most sense for your life. Express gratitude. A little can go a long way. You should try to shoot for something used – maybe 2-4 years old – so that it's less expensive to *insure* once you leave the nest and start taking care of your own financial life.

You should shoot for something relatively fuel-efficient, so it's less expensive to *drive* as well. If your parents get you a used Honda Civic or Nissan Leaf or Kia Soul or something like that when you're 17ish, plan on driving and maintaining that thing until you're 25 at least. It will provide a tremendous economic advantage over someone who has to figure out how to arrange their own ride.

All of this said, we're old people, and we know that this conversation is hardly likely. We would have taken a brand-new car when we were 16, too.

. . .

Kid Pays for Car

The second option is to go out and buy a car all on your own.

For many families, this is really the only option – if the kid wants a car, the kid goes out and earns the money to pay for the car, and that's that.

As a note to any parents who might be reading this, we don't recommend going any further into debt to get your teen a car. It's hardly irresponsible parenting to tell (and show) a teen to take on the responsibility of earning enough money for a car purchase.

We'll discuss the economic implications of car buying in more detail as we continue.

Some Combination of Parent and Kid

In our experience, this is the most common, and perhaps the most financially workable option. Here, the kids and parents work *together* to obtain the car. We realize it's a horrifying thought, but you'll likely survive a few moments of teamwork with your folks.

What's more, it's usually more financially workable because of all the additional expenses that are associated with a car purchase. There's *much* more to it than simply handing over a check at a dealership. But more about that later.

There are literally hundreds of possibilities when teaming up to buy a car. Here is just one scenario:

Before shopping even begins, the parents and teen set the budget for the car's price. Let's say that the agreed number is $8,000. Parents and teen then determine how that figure will be split. Let's assume a 50/50 split of the cost.

Obviously, this means that the teen would need to save $4,000 for the car, and then the parents could match with the other $4,000. (Note to parents: consider setting a limit on what you commit to matching.)

Maybe that seems like a lot to spend on a car. Maybe that seems like not very much. The larger point is that you will now have a *plan* for getting your transportation, and you will have lots of options at your fingertips.

At the time of this writing, there are over 500 matches for cars that are between $6000 and $8000 within a 50-mile radius of where we live. An $8k budget will let you get a used Mini Cooper, a Ford Focus, Honda Civic, Toyota Camry, or a high mileage pickup, and even an 11-year-old Mercedes C class if you're feeling froggy. My first car was an absolute beater, but yours doesn't have to be.

The reason we picked an $8,000 car for this illustration – which would be $4,000 of savings for the teen – is that this should be a workable amount for most. This represents working *roughly* 10 hours a week at $10 per hour, and then being able to save all that money for one year.

When put into those terms, it doesn't sound too bad, does it? You can work 10 hours a week, right? You can save most of that for a year, right?

Plus, most parents will feel better about the car purchase knowing exactly how much you'll be contributing towards the effort. "I need a car now, mom," is one thing. "I need a car and want to contribute $4,000. Can we talk more about it?" is quite another. Every single parent on the planet will react better to the latter than the former.

This discussion of working and saving money now brings us to the chicken-and-egg conundrum when it comes to buying a car: How are you supposed to work part time and save 100 bucks (or so) a week when your work is 3 miles from your house or apartment?

Well, first of all, 3 miles isn't all that far to bicycle.

Second of all, if you must have a car for work – it's more than a few miles and/or you have to haul work-associated gear – then we're entering the world of car loans and car payments.

The Target Car Payment: Zero

The first rule of car loans for teens and young adults is not to have a car loan.

Period.

If you can pay for a car in full up front, you will save yourself hundreds, if not thousands of dollars. Plus, you will experience a deep sense of accomplishment every time you sit in that car. You will be justifiably proud that you have worked and saved, will treat the car differently, and will be better off in the long run in so many ways when compared to someone who is just handed the keys to a new car just for managing to roll out of bed on the day they turn 16. This is more than Chet can say about his new Jeep, and it will show in Chet's behavior and self-image... you'll just have to trust us on that one.

In any event, if you simply can't save money to pay the full cost upfront, you'll need to figure out how to *finance* that car.

If You Focus on the Payment, You're Doing it Wrong

As we've seen, car buying can be a chicken-and-egg conundrum where you can't buy a car without working, and you can't get to work without car. So, you need a loan.

But the chicken-and-egg thing gets even worse: you have trouble getting a loan because you don't have a credit history.

Our advice, when and if you need to start shopping for car loans, is to start by shopping for the *money* first. The absolute worst time and place to figure out how to pay for a car is while you're in the dealership and have already picked out a ride. Dealers will do everything they can to get you financed for a car purchase, even if it means getting you into a loan that's very expensive in terms of either the interest rate or the term. That's because after you sign the papers and drive the car off the lot, it's not their problem anymore – they'll have gotten their money from the bank issuing the loan.

Instead, our recommendation is to start your car shopping at your bank, a credit union, or even your insurer. Often, the company that insures your car will have a department that can finance all or some of the vehicle cost.

Which brings us back to the parents, and the likely possibility that you will have to work with your folks to get that first car. In most instances, you'll need someone with a credit and employment history to *cosign* your loan. The loan cosigner doesn't *have* to be your parents, but as this person (or persons) is responsible for making payments on the loan in the event that you cannot, it almost always is.

And even when you finance the car through the bank or credit union, they will often require some kind of *down payment.*

Why? Because it shows that you have some skin in the game. You're gonna need to work and budget some money to afford the ongoing car payments. The down payment is an indicator that you are bringing this capability to the table; that you have some measure of what it takes to be a responsible, car-owning adult.

In addition, the more you can put down towards the price of the car, the lower your monthly payments will be.

And we can't emphasize this enough: your goal in monthly payments for your car **should be zero.**

Shopping for the loan before shopping for the car, the focus will be on the three most important factors that will impact the cost of the car:

- the **total** price of the car
- the **interest rate** of the loan
- the **length** of the loan

Dealers who want you to take a car off their lot will often talk only about the monthly payment. As you will see in just a moment, the same monthly payment can mean wildly different bottom-line prices, a fact which can make the car buying process very confusing, and a fact that dealers will leverage to their own advantage.

But if you only focus on the monthly payment, you're doing it wrong.

To illustrate, let's start with this… when it comes to car buying, which of these two options offers the more attractive price:

$7,600 or $10,000?

You are getting smarter about money, so of course $7,600 is the more attractive price.

More attractive by $2,400 to be exact.

But in terms of a monthly car payment, these two total prices can be paid for with a monthly payment of **$230 per month.**

The difference? The length of the loan. $230 a month borrowed at 4.9 percent lets you buy a $7,600 car financed for 36 months (3 years), or a $10,000 car financed for 48 months (4 years).

Yeah, but I don't care about paying for another year, you say. *I mean $230 a month is $230 a month, amirite?*

That's a perfectly acceptable counterargument. This isn't really a matter of right vs. wrong in this case, but rather a matter of making an informed decision by understanding that a monthly car payment can confuse, rather than clarify, the decision about a car.

In terms of 36 months vs. 48 months: a year is a long time to pay for something. And you can use the $230/month for a year to pay for other things. Like an education. Or a home. (Or sometimes even a child.) Believe us, when you're starting out in life, there will be <u>no</u> shortage of things to spend $230 on every month.

Besides, what do you anticipate doing three years from now? If you're a junior in high school, you might be a freshman attending college in three years. You're going to be making an entirely new life for yourself, forging new friendships, facing a more demanding class load, and living on your own for what is likely the first time. How easy is it going to be *then* to come up with $230 every month?

Therefore, the one thing that you can do that will probably have the greatest immediate financial impact on your life during your teens and early 20s is to spend the <u>least</u> amount of your money as possible on safe, reliable transportation.

And we haven't even touched on interest rates yet. Another thing that focusing on monthly payments alone can cause people to miss is the interest rate on the loan. You can be paying $230 per month for your car, but if you have a bad credit score, the interest rate on that loan might be as high at **25%.**

Let us repeat that. It is perfectly legal in this country, unfortunately, to charge interest rates of *25%* for used car loans. In the $230/month scenario we've outlined here, that means that you'll be driving around in a $7,000 car, and paying **$4,000 in interest** to the lender, which means you'll have paid $11,000 for a $7,000 car.

Many of these low credit score/high interest rate loans have required minimums. CapitalOne, to take just one brand-name example, has one such product for borrowers with a minimum credit score of only 540, but the minimum loan amount is $7500. So, the $4,000 cost to buy a $7,000 car is a very real-life possibility. Don't do it. Figure out how to buy a $4,000 car. Don't buy a $7,000 car and pay someone else $4,000 in financing costs.

There are thousands of rich people in this country who drive $100,000 luxury cars by selling $5,000 pile of junk cars[2] to poor people because they don't understand the significance of that monthly payment number.

So now that <u>you</u> understand, just ask yourself if you'd rather have $4,000 to spend on something else, or do you prefer to hand it over to the people who sold you the car?

The bottom line here is that getting you to focus only on the monthly payment is literally the oldest car dealer trick in the book. It's how they get you to buy more expensive (and more profitable for them) cars. It's how they get you to pay higher interest rates, which means compound interest for them at rates they couldn't dream of getting if investing in the stock market. In short, it's the trick car dealers have been using for 100 years to separate people from their hard-earned dollars.

Our recommendation, then, is that you never, *ever*, finance for more than 48 months. If you can't afford the payment monthly at 48 months, you can afford the car.

Beyond that, a 36-month loan term is better than 48-month. And a 24-month loan is better than 36. 12 beats 24.

And the best car loan term of all? Zero months.

Your Strategy for Car Buying for the Next 10-12 Years

Until you reach, oh, let's say your 30s, and have a steady income and a few kids of your own who you want to plop in the back of your SUV or minivan, there is virtually no better way to undermine all your other wealth-building efforts than by plowing your money into a car.

But the good news is that it's actually very simple to create a plan so that we don't make big mistakes when it comes to cars.

Even better, the plan has already been made for us!

In his book *The Millionaire Teacher: The Nine Rules of Wealth You Should Have Learned in School*, author Andrew Hallam spends a great deal of time on the subject of car purchases in his very first chapter.

And while Meri and I don't wholeheartedly recommend the entire book – it's focused a little too much on absolutes, of which there aren't very many in the financial business – we do happen to agree with his autobiographical advice on buying cars (and even selling them for a profit later on). Note that the emphasis used in this excerpt is ours.

"… Over the next few years, I bought several low-mileage, reliable Japanese models. I paid between $1,500 to $5,000 for each car. In most cases, I drove them for at least 12 months without putting any extra money into them. My cars were cheap, so my profits didn't amount to much, usually $800 to $1,000 a car. ***Unfortunately, there are too many people who aren't good with money.*** *It's often easy to find desperate people who have overextended themselves financially.* ***Buy from them.*** *Generally, they want money quickly, either to upgrade their cars* ***or to pay off oppressively looming debts.***

I've bought used vehicles from both types of sellers, put as many as 60,000 miles on the cars, and then sold them two or three years later for the same price I paid. On one occasion, I bought a low-mileage, 12-year-old Toyota van for $3,000. I drove it 4,000 miles from British Columbia, Canada, down the Mexican Baja peninsula, then on to Guadalajara, before driving back to Canada. After covering more than 8,000 miles in a single trip, I sold it for $3,500.

Here's one surprisingly simple strategy for buying used vehicles that can save you loads of time and money.

… first, I identify exactly what I'm looking for. A few years ago, I wanted a Japanese car with a stick shift and original paint. I didn't want a new paint job because I'm not skilled enough to determine whether something had been covered up, such as rust or damage from an accident. I also wanted to ensure that the car had fewer than 80,000 miles on it, and I wanted to pay less than $3,000. It really didn't matter how old the car was as long as it had been properly maintained and hadn't been around the block too many times.

Like a secret agent wrapped up in the bravery of anonymity, I pulled out my hit list from the yellow pages to call every car lot within a 20-mile radius. Sticking to my guns, I told them exactly what I was looking for. I wouldn't entertain anything that didn't fit my criteria.

I did have to hold my ground with aggressive sales staff. But it was a lot easier to do over the telephone than it would have been in person. Most of the dealers told me that they had something I would be interested in, but they couldn't go as low as $3,000. Some tried tempting me into their lairs with alternatives; others referred to my price ceiling as delusional. But I wasn't bothered. My strategy was a knight's sword and the phone, my trusty shield. I also practiced chivalry—knowing that I might end up calling on them again.

Because my first round of phone calls didn't pan out, I called the dealers back when it got closer to the end of the month. I hoped the salespeople would be hungrier by then to meet their monthly quotas. As fortune would have it, at one dealership an elderly couple had traded in an older Toyota Tercel with 30,000 miles on it. The car hadn't been cleaned or inspected, but the dealership was willing to do a quick turnaround sale for $3,000.

This strategy doesn't have to be limited to a $3,000 purchase. The process makes sense for any make or model and it saves time. Over the past five years, I've become far less extreme. I no longer pinch pennies. But I still buy used cars. Typically, I now sell them for a little less than what I paid. But if I add up all the money that I've "lost" on cars over the past five years, it doesn't amount to much. **The typical new car buyer will lose more money in five months than I've lost in five years. If you save more money on cars, you can invest more money in wealth-building assets."**

All the Other Stuff We Tend Not to Consider

The out-the-door price won't be the only thing that determines how much you'll need to set aside for the pleasure of getting to and from your place of employment (and maybe even a road trip with friends during Spring Break).

It's very easy to forget about the <u>added</u> expenses that come with owning a car, such as the cost of fuel, maintenance, and insurance, along with state and property taxes which will vary from state to state.

To make the matter of a car purchase an even more costly proposition, many of these costs, such as titling and registering your car, are due within the first 30 days.

I know. Welcome to adulthood.

Titling the Car

How do I prove that I own a car? The fact that it's sitting in my driveway?

Well, what if I stole the car? The car would still be in my driveway, right? So does that change who the owner of the vehicle is?

Questions like these are answered with the car's *title*.

A vehicle title refers to a legal document that provides the **proof of ownership** of a vehicle. You will need the title of a car for different situations. A title contains important information about your car, like the Vehicle Identification Number, the mileage, and the date in which the title was issued. It contains other information that can vary from state to state.

And for purposes of our discussion here, the title also contains the name and address of the owner of the vehicle.

When a vehicle is bought and sold, the seller signs the title, in effect saying, *"Here, I affirm with my signature that I no longer own the car."* Meanwhile, the buyer also signs the title, saying in effect, *"Here, I own this car now, and will register it with the state where I live, and maintain insurance so that any damage I cause while operating the vehicle will be covered."*

When you go to buy a car from a dealership, they will take care of getting the title to you. Your job, then, is to take that title to the Department of Vehicles in your state to get your vehicle properly *licensed* and *registered*. Simply put, the state wants (and needs) to keep track of who owns which cars.

That way, if I steal your car, and it ends up in my driveway, when the cops come by to question me, they can say, *"Now look here, bub, according to our records, that car actually belongs to someone else."* OK, fine, they wouldn't use the word "Bub."

And perhaps the most relevant part of the titling conversation is this:

You will pay a fee to register the car with the state, as you are required to do. Doesn't matter if it's a new car or used. So, remember to factor that into the cash you'll need up front when buying your first car.

Sales Tax

As you know, in most states, a $2 soft drink at the grocery store isn't $2. It's $2 plus whatever the state and local governments have decided to charge in sales tax. Now let's see if we can guess how that relates to the car buying process, shall we?

Yeah. In most states, you'll pay state and local sales taxes on cars, too.

Up front. Usually paid when you go to register the car.

Sometimes the taxes can be rolled into the car loan payments. But keep in mind that this isn't the case in all states, so ask!

And it can be a real kick in the... mid-section... when you get that bill.

For example, the combined sales tax rate for cars registered in Johnson County, Kansas (home of Kansas City and several of its suburbs) is 7.975 percent. That means that if you – or your parents – go buy a $30,000 car, which is less than the average of a new car today, you will have to fork over $2,277 when you go to get the car licensed with the state.

A full rundown of state-by-state taxation is beyond what we can cover here. For example, Montana doesn't have a state car sales tax. So, if you're one of the dozen or so people who lives in Montana, congratulations! No car tax for you! Oh, and Arkansas: If the car is under $4,000 then it's also tax-free.

Hooray, Arkansas!

But otherwise, the big takeaway– and believe us, this is a big one – is that the car buying process can be accompanied by a hefty tax bill at the moment you buy the car, and that has to be paid with out-of-pocket cash.

So ask! Factor it in to your calculations!

Your bank or credit union loan officer will be an expert in this sort of thing. They will know exactly how much you will owe for any given purchase price of car. They will be able to tell whether the taxes can be rolled into the loan, or whether you'll be on your own to cough up an extra couple hundred dollars when buying the car.

COST OF INSURANCE

The last consideration that goes into the price of a vehicle is the cost of legally operating it. Although sales tax liabilities can vary from state to state, every single state in the United States, along with every single country on Earth that we're aware of, requires its drivers to carry *liability* insurance.

The reason why insurance is the law of the land is because you can do a lot of damage to property and other persons from behind the wheel of the car. If someone hits you while driving a car, they need to make you whole. They need to repair your vehicle, and are also responsible for any medical bills you might incur.

A full discussion of car insurance, and how it relates to teenagers, could easily fill up another chapter of this book. Our purpose here is simply to remind you that the cost of insurance needs to be factored into the monthly costs of owning a vehicle. Simply put, car insurance for teenagers is not cheap. Often, monthly insurance premiums are more than the payment for the car itself.

To illustrate, throughout this chapter we've been using a hypothetical monthly car payment of $230 per month.

According to a source called QuoteWizard,[3] the *average* cost of adding a 16-year-old to a parent's insurance policy in 2018 was $270 per month.

And for a teenager who is securing their own standalone insurance policy? The average rate is a somewhat staggering $438 dollars per month.

Why? It's because young drivers pose a huge risk to auto insurers. Drivers between the ages of 16 and 19 are nearly three times more likely to be involved in a fatal crash, are more likely to speed, and have the lowest rate of seatbelt use when compared to other age groups according to the Centers for Disease Control and Prevention (the CDC).

So that's why.

Insurance numbers like these have Meri and I eagerly looking forward to the day when autonomous-driving electric vehicles become commonplace throughout the world, and people can get from Point A to Point B without having to choose between food and transportation. Plus, autonomous cars will be a lot safer. Most of us adult types will feel a lot better about you texting in a car as long as you're not texting while driving the car. We feel the same ways about adults who do the same thing.

In any event, we're recommending a conversation with your parents or guardian about insurance possibilities. As we have just seen, teens can obtain *much* lower rates when bundled with their parent's insurance plans than they otherwise could if they were to buy insurance on their own.

A Word on Leasing

No.

That's the word on leasing.

Paul and I know a few of our friends who lease vehicles, but in almost every case, buying a car is a better financial decision than leasing one.

Under a lease, drivers can often afford a more expensive car, but the tradeoff is that you're merely renting the car, and you won't get anything for it when it's time for a different one.

Unless you have an employer who provides you a car allowance as a perk of the job (and stipulates that whatever you get is their car, not yours), or if you need to utilize several cars for your business to operate – maybe several trucks used for a tree service business, or several vans for a delivery business – then the math says that buying is better than leasing.

Why?

Again, the main reason is that a lease means you're *renting* the car.

Want more reasons? Fine, here are three other significant disadvantages to leasing.

- **You still pay for gas and (most) maintenance.** Some leases will offer lifetime (the lifetime of the lease, that is) oil changes, and you should be covered for any major mechanical defects while you are renting the new car for 2-3 years, but you'll still need to buy gasoline. You'll still need to rotate the tires. Or get new ones.
- **You may pay for the miles driven.** Look carefully at the fine print of advertised car leases. (Actually, don't even consider leasing in the first place.) Many leases have mileage enticements that will have you paying out of pocket for mileage over a certain threshold, which is usually low.
- **You start back at square one.** At the end of car ownership, you have an asset that you can try and sell to someone else. Even if the car won't start and has to be towed from your driveway, someone will usually offer you a few hundred bucks so they can sell it for parts in a junkyard.

And failing even that, you can usually find a charity to whom you can donate the car, and take a deduction from your federal taxes. Even if it's $100... a hundred bucks is a hundred bucks.

In fact, getting into the habit of leasing a car while you're young can put you on a financial hamster wheel that can be very difficult to escape. And it can cost you hundreds of thousands of dollars over your lifetime.

Again, advice on car leasing from *The Millionaire Teacher:*

"Nathan,[4] *like most wealthy people, tracks what he spends. He and his wife's two cars cost them about $2,200 a year after calculating purchase price, maintenance costs, and resale value. The difference between buying low-cost, low-mileage used models versus leasing is about $4,856 a year for a two-car household.*

The US stock market averaged a compound annual return of 9.2 percent from January 1990 through July 2016. If a couple invested $4,856 a year, and if they earned such a return, they would make a lot of money.

...over 15 years this investment would earn them $158,162. Over 35 years, they would have more than $1 million. That's why Nathan says that leasing cars is a $1-million decision."

The takeaway is that when you lease, you get zilch-o when the lease is over. When you buy, you can get zilch-o in terms of your car payment, plus you get to keep the car!

Oh, and when you return your leased car, you also usually get the pleasure of a high-pressure sales pitch from the dealer. They know they have you in a vulnerable position – what are you gonna do, *walk* home from the car lot? Yes, you usually have the option to buy the car you've been leasing, at which point it becomes just another used car transaction. For the most part, all the money you've spent in monthly payments over the years may as well have been burned as fuel for the car.

And just in case we haven't made the case clearly enough, know that leases aren't typically available to people under 18.

So, yeah... if you're a teen, or if you're most every adult, don't lease a car.

Ever.

Final Thoughts

We know what you're thinking: the last thing you need is more homework.

But think of buying a first car as a chance to apply all those homework skills to achieving one of your real-life goals. By researching options before you buy, you'll have a much better chance of finding a car that you can afford, and that is a good fit for your life.

And as you know, there's a wealth of car information that's always a few thumb taps away, so there's no excuse for not being fully prepared to make the best possible deal for your budget.

Here are a few sites that can help you evaluate what's out there in terms of cost to buy the car, and cost to maintain and insure the car.

Cars.com: Search cars near you by body type, transmission type, engine power, and more. It also provides user review of car makes and models. You can also quickly list a car for sale on Cars.com.

AutoTrader: Very similar to Cars.com, AutoTrader lets you search inventory and filter choices by make, model, year, color, style, mileage, and more. You can also sell cars here.

CarGurus: CarGurus provides car reviews and photos from real people. CarGurus shows current prices and compares them with the reported market value of the car to indicate whether or not the listed car is a good deal, fair deal, or bad deal.

Edmunds: Use this tool to search by an extensive range of features like keyless ignition and navigation systems, as well as by price and fuel efficiency.

Consumer Reports: Get safety and reliability information from the national leader in product analysis and information.

Kelley Blue Book: This trusted resource highlights reviews and recommendations for every class of car and offers more tools to help you research your options.

fueleconomy.gov: Research fuel efficiency ratings for the cars on your list with this official government site.

The information available at these sites and apps will help you narrow down your choices before you take that test drive. Remember that a car that looks appealing in the listing may not handle as you expect it to. It's important to test drive at least three vehicles of the same model so you can learn how performance can vary from vehicle to vehicle.

And a final pro tip: One of the best ways to get a great price on a car is to have dealers compete against one another. It shouldn't be too hard to find three cars of the exact same make and model in your local area. Tell each dealer that you're buying, for example, a black Ford Focus hatchback, get a quote from one, and then use that number to negotiate for a better bargain.

CHAPTER SEVEN

NOW WHAT? INVESTING FOR NOW AND FOREVER

How to be a Millionaire (When You Retire)

I n this chapter, we'll show you a strategy to save $2,500,000 for retirement. Even better, this cool hypothetical $2.5 million can be accumulated just by setting aside a small amount each month.

How does that work?

Here are the assumptions we plugged into the moneychimp.com compounding interest calculator:

- **Current Principle: $0**
- **Monthly contribution:**
- Age 19 to 29: $250/m
- Age 30 to 39: $500/m
- Age 40 to 49: $1,000/m
- Age 50 to 59: $2,000/m
- Age 60 to 67: $3,000/m
- **Growth rate: 6%**

Now, here's how this works. Each month save per the list above. As you get older you will make more money which means you can save more money. By age 67 you have saved \$2,572,859. So, steady savings, compounding growth, will give you a nice retirement savings account to retire on.

Now, then: there's one very significant variable in the compound interest calculator that we haven't touched on in much detail yet. It's that interest rate.

How will the money grow at 6%?

Growing the money is done by *investing* it.

Fortunately, the rules for investing as a young person are ridiculously simple. In fact, many of the common strategies that most people need can easily fit into single chapter. And by the time you're done with this chapter, you'll be exposed to two important *whats* that you need to know when you're starting out in your investing life.

You'll know what kind of *account* to open for your path toward millionaire status, and what kinds of *investments* that can be used in those accounts.

Financial Advice Will Always Be Necessary. The End.

Financial *advice*, from financial advisors will also always be necessary. But the younger you are the less lightly you need one. There will always be individuals that don't want to understand stocks and bonds; or spend anytime creating a retirement plan. There will also be individuals who can figure out their risk tolerance and match it with an appropriate asset allocation. Where you fit will be what interests you the most.

But at a young age (under 30 years old) a purchase and hold strategy works just fine.

How much risk an individual can tolerate determines your percentages in stocks and bonds. If you can handle a lot of risk (i.e. large swings in the stock market), you could have an asset allocation that is made up of 100% stocks. On the other hand, if you can't tolerate large swings in the stock market, you could have an asset allocation of 100% bonds. This is an answer specific to you and only you. Don't look at your neighbor and copy his ideas, you need to understand your own risk.

For now, the thing to know is that when we open up our first accounts and start to buy things like index funds, we will have to make a choice about which *type* of account to open.

The options can be a bit confusing, but that's what Meri and I have been put on this planet to do: un-confuse things so that you know which kind of account may suits your needs.

The IRA Account

By far the most popular type of account used to help people save for later in life is something called and Individual Retirement Account – the IRA. The bargain of the IRA account (even though it's technically redundant to say "IRA account," this is how most use the phrase. I guess it's because say some might say "Ira" rather than pronounce the individual letters.[1]) is that it reduces your tax liability today, in exchange for paying taxes later on.

As such, IRAs[2] are known as *pre-tax* investment accounts. These types of accounts were introduced as a way for the government to offset some of their liability on future retirees in the form of Social Security benefits (recall from Chapter 5 that Social Security is when that FICA guy starts paying you back once you reach age 67 or so.)

The 401(k)

A 401(k) is a subset of an Individual Retirement Account that is offered by employers as part of their benefit package. Like the *individual* IRA, this is type of IRA that's intended to help employees save for retirement.

Simply put, a 401(k) is an IRA offered through an employer.

What's more, 401(k) plans often include something known as a *company match*, which simply means that if you save in your 401(k), the company will also contribute a percentage or dollar amount to the 401(k) plan. If the company match is 100% for example, a $300 investment becomes $600 instantly This is effectively a 100% return on investment.

Never, ever, *ever* turn down an opportunity to make free money.

Always, always, always consider contributing to a 401(k) at a rate that will maximize your company's match. What companies do will vary – some match 50% of the first 5% of your contribution; some companies won't match any amount – but the bottom line is that if your company offers a match, you should do everything in your power to maximize that match. Not maxing your company 401(k) match is like not bending down to pick up a $20 bill you find on the front step of your house or apartment. When free money comes along, it's probably a good idea to accept it.

After maxing a 401(k) company match, what else should you consider? **Roth IRA.**

But what's a Roth IRA, you ask?

The Roth IRA

Introduced into the financial landscape as part of the Taxpayer Relief Act of 1997, Roth IRAs were the brainchild of a congressman from Delaware named William Roth. The idea behind this type of individual retirement account was that if the government allowed people to save money for retirement, with the promise of not having to pay taxes on that money when it was being withdrawn, such an account would incentivize even more Americans to subsidize their existing retirement savings.

In other words, the Roth IRA is pretty much the opposite of the IRAs and 401(k)s. With a Roth, you get taxed today, but don't get taxed in the future.

So, let's cut to the chase: which type of account is better for the 19-year-old who wants to save $150/month today, so they can do snow angels in their stacks of cash later on?

In many cases, it's the Roth.

Why? Because when you're young, and you're not making very much money in the first place, then the taxes on those wages aren't going to be terribly significant. In fact, as we detailed earlier, you're likely to get some, if not all, of your federal taxes paid back when you file your return.

Then, when you're older and are taking $50,000 or more out of those same accounts every year, not paying taxes on those withdrawals can make a substantial difference to your monthly income. If you withdraw $50,000 from a regular IRA, and you're in a 30% tax bracket you could owe about $15,000 of that in taxes. If you withdraw $50,000 from a Roth IRA, that's $15,000 you get to spend however you like.

See? Big difference.

Maximizing the 401(k) contribution to take advantage of a possible company match, and then continuing to make contributions to a Roth IRA can lead to a great start in retirement income planning.

Taxable Accounts

You can also store investments in a regular, taxable brokerage (or bank) account.

This designation means that the assets in these kinds of accounts don't enjoy either present or future tax benefits. Another descriptor used for regular brokerage accounts is that they are *non-qualified*, meaning that they aren't qualified for any tax benefits.

One of the more common examples of this type of non-qualified account would be any savings you have at the bank. If the account earns interest, then that interest is taxable each year. However, given the interest rates paid by savings accounts, factoring any taxable income from savings accounts is not a worthwhile exercise. In most cases, we're talking about just a few bucks a year.

The advantage – and indeed the purpose – of a savings account is that it provides quick access to cash. For example, if your car breaks down and you're faced with a $500 car repair, then the savings account provides immediate access to the $500 (provided you have that much in your account, of course).

For this reason, many people refer to savings accounts as *emergency savings* funds. Emergency savings are a great idea, when you're young the amount needed may be less than at an older age. While you're in your 20s, you want that money invested and growing at higher interest rates.

So now that we've looked at what type of account you might open —let's now look at what type of *investment* that account might contain.

Investing in Equities

For the purposes of this discussion, an *equity* is a share of a stock in a publicly traded company. When you buy a share of stock, you are purchasing partial ownership of the company whose stock you're buying. The idea of a stock share is that it represents the portion of the money that would be returned to a company's *shareholders* if all of the assets were liquidated and all of the company's debt was paid off.

For example, if you held a single share of the McDonald's Corporation stock, and suddenly McDonalds were to liquidate – if they were to sell off all of the French fry machines in all of their restaurants, and also sell off all of the land those restaurants sat on, then the McDonald's Corporation would then have one rather substantial pile of money. That money would then be divided by several million shares and so you, as a shareholder, would get 1/525 millionth of that pile of money.

If that sounds like a good deal, it's not. A better outcome for you as owner of the share of McDonald's stock would be for McDonald's to continue to grow their business by opening new stores, or selling more hamburgers, Shamrock shakes, and chicken nuggets with that delicious Szechuan sauce.[3] Then, because of all of this improved business, the overall value of the company increases, and thus the perceived value of your shared ownership of that company likewise increases. You could then offer your share of McDonald's stock for sale at a special kind of marketplace known as a *stock exchange*.

As you may already know, the most well-known examples of stock exchanges in the United States are the New York Stock

Exchange and the NASDAQ (an acronym that stands for National Association of Securities Dealers Automated Quotations).

And to clear up a common misconception about stock markets, it's the place where buyers and sellers of part ownership of a company (i.e. shares) get together to buy and sell those shares. When you buy a share of stock, the company doesn't receive your money – the seller of the share gets your money. The only time the company gets the money you're exchanging for part ownership of the company is during the initial public offering of the shares.

In any event, here's the truly difficult part about choosing to purchase part ownership of a single company like McDonald's: you don't have a time machine or a crystal ball.

If you had either of these two devices, perhaps you could travel (or see) 10 years into the future and report back about the health of the McDonald's Corporation 10 years from now. Are they continuing to open up restaurants? Are the hamburgers more delicious and more popular than ever before? Or has there been some development that has adversely affected the profitability of McDonald's? Is there a worldwide shortage of beef? Did Wendy's sign an exclusive deal with Beyond Meat which has made Wendy's a lot more popular with millennials (or whatever we'll call millennials 10 year from now)? Have preferences changed, making the street taco more popular in most U.S. cities than the hamburger?

The point is that we don't have a crystal ball. The point is that McDonald's could be more valuable in 10 years, it could be less valuable, or it could remain exactly as valuable as it is today, no more and no less.

The same holds true for any publicly traded company. People love to make predictions based on the information they have today, but the future value of any company will be based on information that will only become available sometime in the future. For example, how many iPhones will Apple sell in the year 2021? Analysts can make predictions, but it's 2020 today, and we won't know exactly how many iPhones will be sold in the year 2021 until 2021 actually gets here and Apple counts up how many phones it sold.

It may be reasonable to *assume* that Apple will sell hundreds of millions of iPhones between now and then, but it's always helpful to remember that people were saying same thing about BlackBerries in 2008. You know how many iPhones analysts were saying Apple would sell in 2005? Trick question! In 2005, the iPhone didn't exist.

Buying a Mutual Fund

If buying one stock seems too risky, one of your options is to purchase shares of a **mutual fund.**

A mutual fund pools money from lots of different investors – let's imagine 10,000 people who are contributing $150 per month into a Roth IRA – and then uses that pool of $1.5 million every month to then buy <u>many</u> different stocks. Depending on the mutual fund manager, the fund may also purchase assets such as bonds. (More about bonds in just a bit.)

Just as with the price of individual stocks like Apple or McDonalds, pieces of a mutual fund are bought and sold as shares, and these shares rise or fall in value based on the performance of the fund's underlying assets.

When you invest in a mutual fund, the value of your investment can grow in one of three ways:

Dividend payments. When a fund receives dividends or interest from the stocks and bonds in which it invests, this income is returned to mutual fund shareholders. When you purchase mutual fund shares, you can choose to receive your distributions directly, or have them reinvested in the fund. For a young person, a strategy that reinvests mutual fund dividends and interest may be most beneficial.

Capital gains. The mutual fund managers can, at their discretion, choose to sell a security that's has gone up in price – in fact, the rules of mutual funds is that they <u>have</u> to from time to time. A mutual fund can't have 50% of its assets under management be only Apple stock, for example. When a funds sells shares at a profit, this is known as a **capital gain.** Most funds distribute any net capital gains to investors annually, but again the rule is that these gains should be reinvested.

Net asset value (NAV). As the value of the fund increases, so does the price to purchase a single share of the fund. This is equivalent to having a stock price increase, and is just as desirable for most investors. In almost all instances, you want the share price to increase so that when you sell, you've made a profit on your shares.

One of the major drawbacks of a mutual fund is that you then bear some responsibility to keep tabs on the performance of the person (or team) who's doing all the individual stock and bond picking. It's sorta up to you to read the mutual fund's annual report each year to ensure the manager is sticking to the financial philosophy in which you believe, and that you are satisfied with the fund's holdings.

In practical terms, this means frequently checking the price of the fund in the same way you might check the price of an individual stock. It means a lot of homework comparing between the hundreds and hundreds of available mutual funds. It means measuring the performance of the fund against the performance of benchmarks like the S&P 500. Spoiler alert: Only about *one in 20* large mutual funds beat the performance of market benchmarks.[4]) If you're constantly having to monitor your fund investment, it kind of defeats the whole purpose.

Buying an Index Fund

In our opinion – an opinion that's backed by years of data – the very best kind of mutual fund available to young investors is the **index fund.**

Why? Because an index fund is simply a mutual fund that, instead of paying a portfolio manager to make individual stock and bond selections – a little bit of Apple, a dash of McDonalds, and a dollop each of Verizon, Chevron, Nike, Walmart, and Intel – the choice of stocks is made by whatever committee determines the index in questions. (In case you're wondering, all of the aforementioned stocks are in today's Dow 30, but haven't always been. Obviously, companies like Nike, Walmart, and Intel didn't even exist 100 years ago. The Dow, however, is even older than that. The index was first put together in 1896.)

For example, if you buy a Dow Jones Industrial Average index fund, you're really just handing over the job of managing your money to the editors of The Wall Street Journal, whose editors come up with the list of the Dow 30 each and every year.

To which we say: *Awesome!*

If you buy an S&P 500 index fund, you're really buying an equal amount of all 500 stocks that the folks who run Standard and Poor's include in their index.

To which we say: *Awesome, wow!*[5]

. We don't know with any certainty what an individual company like Intel or Disney (both part of the Dow and the S&P 500) are going to do in the next 10, 20, or 30 years.

But we don't have to. With an *index fund,* we can buy into all 30 companies that make up the Dow, and also divest ourselves of any companies that are removed from the Dow over the next 30 years. It's set it and forget it investing.

It can be a successful investing strategy in the long run.

In fact, arguably the world's most successful investor, Warren Buffet, famously bet $1 million against any hedge fund manager, and a group called Protégé Partners took him up on the bet. (A hedge fund manager, by the way, is someone who charges a lot of money for their ability to convince wealthy people that they, the hedge fund manager, can predict the future. Oh, and a hedge fund is just a mutual fund that can break some of the mutual fund rules to all but *ensure* that the people running hedge funds lose even more money. If a hedge fund wants to invest 50% in Apple stock, they can. Don't feel bad, though. A lot of wealthy people can afford to, and even think it's exciting, to lose many, many thousands of dollars through hedge fund investments, and then complain about the price of postage stamps.)

In any event, the Warren Buffet bet (with proceeds donated to charity) was that an index fund would beat an average of five hedge funds over a 10-year period.

Buffet won the bet.[6]

His pick, a fund which tracks the S&P 100 index (ticker symbol OEX), gained 125.8% over ten years. The five hedge funds, which were hand-picked by Protégé Partners, gained an average of only 36%.

In short, over a 10-year period, the rich hedge fund managers only underperformed what your dog could have gained in the stock market by about 100%. Seriously, hedge fund managers charge millions of dollars for this! Lots of them end up on TV, even! It's a great job if you can get it.

An Exchange Traded Fund

Recent years have given rise to a very popular type of investment known as an ETF, which is an acronym for Exchange Traded Fund. An ETF is just a mutual fund that trades like a share of stock on a stock exchange (like the NYSE or the NASDAQ) throughout the day. Ordinary mutual funds "settle" – that is, calculate their value per share – at the end of every trading day, but both an ordinary mutual fund and an ETF that track the same index will include the same underlying holdings.

For young investors with a 30- or 40-year time horizon, it really doesn't make much difference whether you're investing in a mutual fund or an ETF.

Before we close, a few questions about index funds:

Does it matter whether your Roth holds an indexed mutual fund or an ETF?

Not really, since the performance of each is going to march in lockstep with the index.

Do you have to buy multiple funds or ETFs to diversify your portfolio?

Not really, since the funds are effectively purchasing 30, or 100, or 500 underlying stocks. For young investors, much of the diversification needed is built into the index.

Investing in Fixed Income

Fixed-income investments are assets that are designed to produce *income* for those who *hold* (i.e. have purchased) such assets.

Fixed-income mutual funds are considered low risk investments, in that they typically don't fluctuate as much in price from month to month and year to year, but the safety comes at a price. Typically, fixed-income investments return somewhere between 4% and 6% per year, sometimes less. In fact, Warren Buffet added an interesting note about bonds in the shareholder letter that summarized his bet vs. hedge fund managers.[7]

Fixed-income investments are used as a diversification tool for many investors' portfolios, but it's a generally not a diversification tool that's needed until we begin to approach retirement age.

Fixed-income assets may not be a consideration until you reach age 50 or so, but if you simply *hate* the thought of seeing the numbers on an annual statement go down from time to time, you may want to consider reducing a bit of your portfolio risk with a small portion in fixed-income. (And even then, the numbers will still go down from time to time; such is the nature of stock markets.)

Usually, this fixed-income investment will be in the form of a bond or fixed-income funds. These funds are simply mutual funds that own fixed-income securities such as U.S. Treasuries, corporate bonds, municipal bonds, and so on.

As with index and other funds and ETFs, fixed-income funds make purchases in <u>many</u> securities, rather than just one. You're thus buying into the returns of all underlying assets.

The way to do that is with index funds that track the world stock markets. That's what Warren Buffet did with his bet, and he beat professional investors by 100% over a ten-year period.

The way <u>not</u> to do that, incidentally, is by chasing "other" kinds of investments.

Final Thoughts

There. I've just told you just about every single thing you need to know about saving your money for later in life. Let's talk again in about 40 years. In another 40 years, you'll need to start factoring things such as Social Security benefits, or required minimum distributions, or tax strategies for passing along money to loved ones and charities.

Until then, I'll leave you with the thoughts of an Internet columnist and knower of financial matters by the name of Hamilton Nolan. I really have no idea who Hamilton Nolan is, but his views expressed here are pretty much in alignment with ours when it comes to investing, and when it comes to advice from certain other financial writers whose names are a lot more well-known that ours.

As always, the emphasis is ours.

"So, the first and most important step to investing your money is to get to the point in life where you have disposable income each month that you can invest. That means first paying off your debts and being able to pay all of your bills. In America, the majority of people never truly make it to this first phase of financial life. Most people never accumulate significant enough excess income to invest in a way that would make a meaningful difference in their lives…

Personal finance skills will never provide financial freedom to the majority of Americans—only systemic economic and social reform resulting in mass redistribution of wealth will do that. So, don't feel too bad if you find yourself wondering why reading a Suze Orman book or whatever seems insufficient to reform your life. The system is the problem.

*That said, **if you do have some extra money you better learn how to invest that shit** because if you think the government is gonna provide for you in your old age you are one overly optimistic fool.*

Maybe you have a 401(k) or other personal investment/retirement plan through your work. Fine, put your money in there, because generally they match it, and that's free money. But to invest your own money, open a Vanguard account. There are a zillion companies that all basically do the same thing, but Vanguard charges you the least, and Vanguard is also owned by its own investors rather than by some rapacious businessman, so its incentive is actually to lower its fees rather than try to raise them. Fees are one of the only things in the financial world you, a nobody, can control. Take advantage.

Open that Vanguard account and you'll see that you can now buy the entire universe of financial products! Stocks, bonds, mutual funds, index funds, ETFs, commodities, REITS, and many other things that you do not understand, if we're being honest. So?

*Is your name Warren Buffett? If so, you should feel free to pick stocks to invest in based upon your own brilliant business insights like "People drink a lot of Coca-Cola these days." **If your name is not Warren Buffett, you should invest in index funds.***

… In the bigger picture, here is the truth of what you are engaging in when you invest your meager nickels in index funds: You are capturing, for yourself, the world's economic growth rate. Without having to do any actual work! The economic growth rate of all the businesses in the world is higher than what you will make by leaving your money under the mattress, and that is why you invest. Rich people figured this out long ago, and this is how they stay rich.

If you, the working person, stick all your cash in a savings account, and Chet, the heir to an evil fortune, puts all his money in the financial markets, Chet's money will grow while yours will not. Investing makes your money grow, whereas saving and spending your money makes it eventually disappear. This is why the Chets of the world will be able to buy a new Jeep for Chet Junior on his sixteenth birthday, even though they do not appear to have real jobs."

In other words, pretty much everything we've just said. (And we told you that we'd eventually get to Chet.)

Call someone like me in 40 years.

If we still have a planet with phone service, that is.

DISCLOSURE

Securities offered through Cambridge Investment Research, Inc., a broker-dealer, member <u>FINRA</u> /<u>SIPC</u> . Investment advisory services offered through Cambridge Investment Research Advisors, Inc., a Registered Investment Advisor. Humphrey Financial LLC and Cambridge are not affiliated.

Licensed Insurance Professional. We are an independent financial services firm helping individuals create retirement strategies using a variety of investment and insurance products to custom suit their needs and objectives. This material has been prepared for informational and educational purposes only. It is not intended to provide, and should not be relied upon for, accounting, legal, tax or investment advice.

NOTES

Chapter 2

1. If this helps make it more palatable, know that you'll also be playing a psychological trick on them. Most people are bothered on a subconscious level by a perceived imbalance. For example, if your friend brings you a candy bar – *even if you didn't ask for a candy bar and don't even like that candy bar* – you're more likely to bring them a doughnut or let them copy your homework than you would have been if the candy bar hadn't been given. You feel some pressure to even out the social scales. Again, this is a subject more for your psychology teacher than your personal finance teacher, but look it up if you don't believe us. Financial advisors treat clients and prospective clients to golf and steak dinners all the time for this very same reason.

   And before you ask: No, this is not to be used for someone you want to ask out. Gifts and favors for possible romantic partners is an entirely different thing. Buying a Frappuccino for someone does not obligate that someone to be your prom date. Cool? Cool.
2. The law also says you have to abide by your parents' instructions while living in their house, so let's not get carried away. You wanna do whatever you want, whenever you want, you gotta first figure out how to move out and pay the first month's rent at your own place.

Chapter 3

1. Source: https://www.cnbc.com/2019/02/21/consumer-debt-hits-4-trillion.html

Chapter 4

1. Source: https://www.investopedia.com/ask/answers/042415/what-average-annual-return-sp-500.asp
2. https://www.thesimpledollar.com/where-does-7-come-from-when-it-comes-to-long-term-stock-returns/
3. http://www.moneychimp.com/features/market_cagr.htm
4. U.S. Department of Labor. https://www.dol.gov/whd/minwage/chart.htm
5. We also would like to acknowledge that gasoline is probably a bad example here. We think it's very, *very* unlikely that you'll even *need* to buy gasoline for cars 30 years from now. Electric vehicles are the future, as they're superior in every way to vehicles that burn gasoline. That's especially true from an economic standpoint. In the long run, EVs are just simply cheaper to own, operate, and refuel. Sometime in the next 10 years, humans will be getting the majority of their electrical

needs met through solar and wind sources, and not because they are "green," but because they're the cheapest way of powering our stuff.

Now, we're not saying that the best economic choice today is to go out and buy a new electric car. We're saying that the data suggests that as of late 2019, we're just beginning a crossover period where personal transportation will shift from gasoline-powered to electricity-powered. Kind of an exciting time, in our opinion. Anyway, if it helps, think in terms of a gallon of milk rather than a gallon of gas.

6. i.e. broke. What are we, your English teachers now?
7. The full list of what the U.S. Bureau of Labor Statistics tracks in calculating the CPI can be found here: https://data.bls.gov/cgi-bin/surveymost

Chapter 5

1. For the purposes of this chapter, all deities that either appear or are invoked somehow on currency, from Zeus to Allah to Yahweh, are being treated as mythical. Throughout human history, we've been ascribing monetary powers to divine beings. Romans prayed to Pluto, and put portraits of Cupid and Jupiter on their money. Egyptians prayed to Horus, and Chinese to Tsai Shen. You get the idea. The only difference now is which deities are commonly invoked.

   In fact, a discussion of the phrase "In God We Trust" could easily fill up another chapter. The phrase did not appear on *any* U.S. money until the country was almost 100 years old, and did not appear on *all* US currency until the Cold War − the phrase was part of a cultural war against communism, which was viewed, by some in the U.S., as a godless threat to Western culture. In any event, the motto, "In God We Trust" is very much a modern construct.
2. You can do the math yourself in just a few seconds at https://www.amortizationtable.org/ Hmm. I smell an assignment coming…
3. This is all from the IRS Publication 929, a 22-page PDF available for your perusal on the IRS website, www.irs.gov. The direct link is here: https://www.irs.gov/pub/irs-pdf/p929.pdf Happy reading, kids!
4. The good news, though, is that you do get it back when you're old − like us! − and ready to file for Social Security benefits, or when your old and in need of medical care, at which time you can visit a Medicare-approved doctor.

Chapter 6

1. You will hear more about Chet in Chapter 7
2. What we're referring to here are cars that were purchased at salvage auction for $1000 and have a myriad of mechanical and structural problems. There are plenty of reliable $5000 used cars available for purchase.
3. https://quotewizard.com/
4. the author's millionaire friend

Chapter 7

1. Although this is just our guess. What are we, your English teachers?
2. That said, IRAs in this context is plural, not possessive, and it drives us crazy to see people write "IRA's" when they really mean "IRAs."
3. Boom! Did that just happen?!? Did we just work in a second *Rick and Morty* reference?
4. Source: https://www.marketwatch.com/story/why-way-fewer-actively-managed-funds-beat-the-sp-than-we-thought-2017-04-24
5. That was a *Hamilton* reference. Perhaps the best argument we can make for invest your money is when invest, you can eventually afford tickets to go see *Hamilton*. It's worth it.
6. You can read more about it here: https://money.cnn.com/2018/02/24/investing/warren-buffett-annual-letter-hedge-fund-bet/index.html
7. Here's the good part, once again from the CNN Business article referenced earlier: "…the "purportedly 'risk-free' long-term bonds" ended up being a "far riskier investment" than common stocks."

ABOUT THE AUTHORS

Meri and Paul Humphrey have been married since 2006, their combined family includes 5 adult kids and 2 grandkids. Meri is a retired music teacher with a lifetime of experiences with all ages of kids. Her dedication to teaching at all levels, helps her to contribute to this book. Paul is still an active financial planner having helped thousands of families with financial planning decisions, starting with college planning and running through retirement planning, and all things planning in between. Meri and Paul have witnessed all forms of financial success and failure, which contributed to this book.